Simply Einstein

Simply Einstein

JIMENA CANALES

SIMPLY CHARLY
NEW YORK

Copyright © 2021 by Jimena Canales

Cover Illustration by Vladymyr Lukash
Cover Design by Scarlett Rugers

All rights reserved. No part of this publication may be reproduced, distributed, or transmitted in any form or by any means, including photocopying, recording, or other electronic or mechanical methods, without the prior written permission of the publisher, except in the case of brief quotations embodied in critical reviews and certain other noncommercial uses permitted by copyright law. For permission requests, write to the publisher at the address below.

permissions@simplycharly.com

ISBN: 978-1-943657-45-2

Brought to you by http://simplycharly.com

Contents

	Praise for *Simply Einstein*	vii
	Other *Great Lives*	xi
	Series Editor's Foreword	xii
	Preface	xiii
	Acknowledgements	xvi
	Introduction	1
1.	A Previously Unknown Physicist Becomes World Famous	3
2.	The Three Classic Tests	20
3.	Einstein's Magical Message	40
4.	Einstein Becomes World Famous	50
5.	Anti-Semitism and Politics	64
6.	Light sees the Light	73
7.	Quantum Mechanics and the Atomic Bomb	81
8.	Skeletons in his Archive	92
9.	Einstein's Legacy	105
	Suggested Reading	109
	About the Author	111
	A Word from the Publisher	112

Praise for *Simply Einstein*

"Jimena Canales is one of the very best contemporary science writers, and no one could have written a clearer, more empathetic or appealing short life of the twentieth century's quintessential scientific genius."
—John Banville, Man Booker Prize-winning author of *The Sea*

"This stimulating book by a distinguished historian of science looks at Einstein from several angles. We see him as the author of the special and general theories of relativity, as an ambitious professor in competition with others, as the exemplar of the brilliant scientist, and as a political figure. We see him as a child, a student, and as a husband and father. Jimena Canales animates the debates about the validity of Einstein's most famous ideas and how they changed our ideas about time and space forever, at their implications for quantum mechanics and the building of the atomic bomb, and at the significance of his legacy today. The book draws on a wide variety of sources to illuminate the impact and the controversies Einstein's work caused and is written throughout in clear and sparkling prose."
—Jeremy Gray, Emeritus Professor, the Open University, U.K. and Honorary Professor of Mathematics, The University of Warwick, U.K.

"*Simply Einstein* offers a succinct and fascinating look at the phenomenal work that made Albert Einstein world-famous. It shows how Einstein's reputation was built on bold theories that were splendidly tested by experiments such as the eclipse expeditions of 1919 and amplified by the media in riveting stories about their revolutionary implications. It offers a great read for those wondering how Einstein vaulted into international fame in the early 20th century and has remained synonymous with genius."

—Paul Halpern, author of *Synchronicity: The Epic Quest to Understand the Quantum Nature of Cause and Effect*

"Jimena Canales captivates us with the tale of how Einstein became "Einstein"—and it's not the story you think. *Simply Einstein* reveals the family, mentors, colleagues, rivals, and lovers who made him into our icon of science. Instead of a lone genius revolutionizing the world, we see him struggling, leaning on his friends, and worrying deeply about how he would be remembered by history. This is the real Einstein—full-blooded and fascinating."

—Matthew Stanley, Professor of the History and Philosophy of Science, New York University

"Like a lotus flower growing in a bog, Einstein's ideas arose, pure and strong as diamond, out of the muck of his personal life and the chaos of his times. The miracle can be neither explained nor emulated; we can only observe it and allow it to inspire us. In this brief biography, Jimena Canales sets out to sketch a fascinating glimpse of Einstein, the man and his legacy, in the hindsight of our own era. Using an expression Einstein used in the title of one of the most consequential papers in the history of science, I am confident that her effort will succeed in its *heuristic* goal of stimulating people to learn and discover on their own"

—Hans Christian von Baeyer, author of *QBism: The Future of Quantum Physics* and Emeritus Chancellor Professor of Physics, College of William & Mary

"Jimena Canales captures the sweep of Einstein's unparalleled career in this engaging biography, revealing how Einstein became an icon. *Simply Einstein* is a captivating introduction to Einstein's most consequential ideas that also invites us to think about scientists' public roles in society today."

—David Kaiser, Germeshausen Professor of the History of

Science and Professor of Physics, Massachusetts Institute of Technology

"Einstein is famous for being an unconventional figure—the hair, the (absence of) socks, sticking out his tongue to photographers—but he is often presented to the public by biographers in a very conventional manner. Jimena Canales's *Simply Einstein* is not conventional. This is an original interpretation of Einstein, studded with quotations and episodes that you will not find in other accounts."

—**Michael D. Gordin**, author of *Einstein in Bohemia* and Rosengarten Professor of Modern and Contemporary History, Princeton University

"By humanizing and situating this larger-than-life figure within the holistic context of physics in the 20th Century, Jimena Canales provides a unique and intriguing understanding of Einstein. She does this by interrogating *how* we know Einstein with how we *should* know Einstein. This is amplified by her gift of writing about the history of science in an engaging manner that serves as a gateway for new entrants into the fascinating subfield of Einstein historians."

—**Tiffany Nichols**, Black Hole Initiative, Harvard University

"In recent years the extraordinary flowering of Einstein scholarship and the new information uncovered about the great man has not necessarily reached the ordinary reader. Jimena Canales' book accessibly introduces a great deal of these exciting historical discoveries to those interested in the man but daunted by the often highly technical aspects of his science. What is particularly good to see is that so much of the story is told through the words of Einstein, his friends and colleagues, and the newspapers and other commentators of the day. The author's great familiarity with the man's life and times shines through in a way that is engaging and engrossing."

—**Daniel Kennefick, author of** *No Shadow of a Doubt: The 1919 Eclipse That Confirmed Einstein's Theory of Relativity*

"Jimena Canales' *Simply Einstein* is a short and quickly paced story that moves through the history of the twentieth century as observed through the lens of Einstein's biography. You get to know Einstein in his place and time as fully part of the cultural and political turmoil of his period."

—**Jeroen van Dongen, Professor of the History of Science, University of Amsterdam**

"Einstein has become, and still is, the worldwide icon of the solitary scientific genius. How did it happen? Award-winning author Jimena Canales succeeds in succinctly conveying to a large readership a de-mythologized image of the man behind the public image Einstein himself endeavored to construct. Wonderfully written and carefully crafted, Canales' succinct biographical sketch not only reveals the humanity, the science, and the mythologizing process of one of last century's most influential scientists, but also invites deep reflection on the changing social role of science through the 20th century."

—**Roberto Lalli, Research Scholar at the Max Planck Institute for the History of Science**

Other *Great Lives*

Simply Austen by Joan Klingel Ray
Simply Beckett by Katherine Weiss
Simply Beethoven by Leon Plantinga
Simply Chekhov by Carol Apollonio
Simply Chomsky by Raphael Salkie
Simply Chopin by William Smialek
Simply Darwin by Michael Ruse
Simply Descartes by Kurt Smith
Simply Dickens by Paul Schlicke
Simply Dirac by Helge Kragh
Simply Eliot by Joseph Maddrey
Simply Euler by Robert E. Bradley
Simply Faulkner by Philip Weinstein
Simply Fitzgerald by Kim Moreland
Simply Freud by Stephen Frosh
Simply Gödel by Richard Tieszen
Simply Hegel by Robert L. Wicks
Simply Hitchcock by David Sterritt
Simply Joyce by Margot Norris
Simply Machiavelli by Robert Fredona
Simply Napoleon by J. David Markham & Matthew Zarzeczny
Simply Nietzsche by Peter Kail
Simply Proust by Jack Jordan
Simply Riemann by Jeremy Gray
Simply Sartre by David Detmer
Simply Tolstoy by Donna Tussing Orwin
Simply Stravinsky by Pieter van den Toorn
Simply Turing by Michael Olinick
Simply Wagner by Thomas S. Grey
Simply Wittgenstein by James C. Klagge

Series Editor's Foreword

Simply Charly's "Great Lives" series offers brief but authoritative introductions to the world's most influential people—scientists, artists, writers, economists, and other historical figures whose contributions have had a meaningful and enduring impact on our society.

Each book provides an illuminating look at the works, ideas, personal lives, and the legacies these individuals left behind, also shedding light on the thought processes, specific events, and experiences that led these remarkable people to their groundbreaking discoveries or other achievements. Additionally, every volume explores various challenges they had to face and overcome to make history in their respective fields, as well as the little-known character traits, quirks, strengths, and frailties, myths, and controversies that sometimes surrounded these personalities.

Our authors are prominent scholars and other top experts who have dedicated their careers to exploring each facet of their subjects' work and personal lives.

Unlike many other works that are merely descriptions of the major milestones in a person's life, the "Great Lives" series goes above and beyond the standard format and content. It brings substance, depth, and clarity to the sometimes-complex lives and works of history's most powerful and influential people.

We hope that by exploring this series, readers will not only gain new knowledge and understanding of what drove these geniuses, but also find inspiration for their own lives. Isn't this what a great book is supposed to do?

Charles Carlini, Simply Charly
New York City

Preface

Adding another line to the preexisting scholarship on Einstein is a daunting challenge for anyone—no matter how well prepared. Thousands of books and articles have been written about arguably history's greatest scientist. The physicist left behind a hefty archival record about his life and work that posterity has painstakingly perused. Renowned scholars have dedicated their entire lives to combing through Einstein's publications, interviews, and public statements, as well as his copious correspondence, unpublished drafts, and numerous other sundry clues that might help us understand this unparalleled genius. Even the circumvolutions of his brain have been an object of intense fascination and speculation. Appropriately nicknamed by *The New York Times* as "the Elvis of science," Einstein still makes it to "Top Earning Dead Celebrities" lists, next to stars such as Elizabeth Taylor, John Lennon, and Michael Jackson. His name and likeness continue to draw annual earnings of millions of dollars.

Partly for these reasons, Einstein remains one of history's most misunderstood scientists. What have we learned about Einstein after studying him for more than a century? More importantly, what have we learned from him about the universe and the capacity of humankind to know it?

Einstein's work is in many senses the story of science in the 20th century, a time when scientists carved out for themselves the prominent place in society they now have. He was not only responsible for the great discoveries he is widely known for, but his most lasting legacy was also forging a new place for science in the modern world.

We now know more about Einstein than ever before. We also know much more about science, its place in society, and how it relates to industry and technology. In recent years, our understanding of how scientific work compares to that of other professions (including those of priests, politicians, and celebrities who create systems of authority and admiration around them) has increased considerably. We know more about how fame and virality function, and how science literacy and education affect our trust in facts and in experts, including Einstein.

A proper answer for how one man obtained such extraordinary success is hard to come by. The challenge, in part, involves separating elements such as talent and ambition from luck and serendipity. It requires making subjective judgments about the importance of an individual's own actions in distinction to those of others close to them, including family, teachers, and friends, and speculating about the relative role played by nature versus nurture. Scholarship on Einstein is rife with conjectures about the respective influence of upbringing, innate psychology, and the broader environment. It is impossible to parse out these elements in fixed and abstract terms across all time and history.

The text that follows is based on an approach that permits us to see Einstein and his work in a new light. It focuses on key aspects of modernity that permitted an otherworldly public figure to emerge from a singular life. The universe discovered by Einstein was a complex four-dimensional structure where nothing could travel faster than light. This same universe also permitted his transformation from an all-too-human patent clerk into an extraordinary icon; it was the birthplace for an extraordinary man who moved in the same historical, social, and political environments as many others. This book, therefore, takes an upside-down approach to the topic: it studies changes that occurred underfoot to understand how our knowledge of the universe changed overhead. To know Einstein thus requires not only searching for the real person behind the myth, but also studying the process of personhood and myth-making that were operative during this period.

My hope is that an appreciation of his life and work deepens when insights are presented in the prosaic ways they first appeared. Thus, we can begin to bring this otherworldly figure back to Earth.

Jimena Canales
Boston, Massachusetts

Acknowledgements

"If you want to sup with the devil, you better use a long spoon." Such advice can serve well those who write about great historical figures.

I first approached "Einstein" cautiously, by probing him from distant angles. My first involvement with his life and work began by studying the 19th-century context that led to his contributions in A Tenth of a Second: A History, a detailed history of time measurements across disciplines from experimental psychology to physics. My second intervention came much closer. The Physicist and the Philosopher: Einstein, Bergson and the Debate that Changed Our Understanding of Time involved studying him alongside one of his most prominent critics. My third venture explored the incredible breadth of his scientific imagination, placing it in the context of other great scientists such as René Descartes, Pierre-Simon Laplace, James Clerk Maxwell, and Charles Darwin, culminating with Bedeviled: A Shadow History of Demons in Science. These three books—the first dealing with the science that preceded Einstein, the second with arguments used against him by his critics, and the third with a history of the imaginary world he inhabited—are the launching pads for this concise biography.

Two previously published articles, in The New Yorker and The Atlantic respectively, dealt with largely unknown aspects of his life. "Albert Einstein's Sci-Fi Stories" explored the source of inspiration of some of his first musings on relativity and "The Secret PR Push That Shaped the Atomic Bomb's Origin Story" centered on Einstein in the immediate aftermath of WWII.

One of the pleasures of writing about this towering figure has been my full immersion in the work of superb scholars and colleagues. Some of these include: Jeroen van Dongen, Peter Galison, Galina Weinstein (previously Granek), Hanoch Gutfreund, Ann and Klaus Hentschel, Gerald Holton, Don Howard, Fred Jerome,

Daniel Kennefick, Alberto Martinez, Katy Price, Jürgen Renn, Tilman Sauer, Richard Staley, and Matthew Stanley. Essential biographical information comes from Michael Gordin, Walter Isaacson, Thomas Levenson, Dennis Overbye, John Stachel, and others.

No original contribution to scholarship is complete without primary source research. The various volumes of *The Collected Papers of Albert Einstein*, edited by Diane Kormos Buchwald and her expert team of annotators and translators, became a permanent fixture on my desk and an endless source of entertainment during the 2020 lockdown. Other compilations and edited volumes (including those by David E. Rowe, Robert Schulmann, Carl Seelig, and others) provided me with additional material. This book remains deeply indebted to their research.

Much more can be said about Einstein (and much more has been said about him already) that can fit in this space. By being highly selective, rather than attempting to be comprehensive, I hope to interest specialists and non-specialists alike. In times of complexity, no virtue is greater than simplicity.

Finally, my gratitude extends to my family, friends, and readers, to whom I dedicate this book.

Introduction

Before the name Albert Einstein became synonymous with genius, an obscure professor of physics labored away for years, rewriting the laws of physics in a completely new way. He had been moderately successful—managing to gain the respect of his peers and climbing the academic ladder—but when British astronomers came back from the solar eclipse expedition of 1919 and analyzed what they saw that day, they confirmed his revolutionary hypothesis. The expedition members eagerly announced to the scientific community and the press that they had caught light bending in ways that could be perfectly explained with Einstein's new theory.

The following day, newspapers ran the story of a rebellious prodigy who had dethroned Isaac Newton by arguing that the universe was four-dimensional, that time and space were no longer absolute, and that they could shrink and expand in unusual ways. The news set experts and the public alike abuzz with excitement, opening up new puzzles and paradoxes.

For the rest of his life, Einstein dedicated himself to promoting his theory and forging a new place for science in society. Privately, he struggled to fit within an oversized public persona which haunted his friendships, love life, and contributions to science. Brilliant, ambitious, and insecure, Einstein remains to this day the ultimate representative of genius.

Einstein revolutionized 20th-century science by upending our traditional understanding of the universe. Arguing that old concepts of time and space were outdated and should be discarded, he crafted a new role for science in the modern world by becoming a celebrity scientist. From his days as a lowly patent clerk to the time when he was hailed by the press and the public for his groundbreaking work in physics, *Simply Einstein* explores the man behind the myth, the process that led to the myth's creation, and the brilliant insights that brought about a new understanding of the cosmos.

This book also tells the story of how an all-too-human scientist became an extraordinary icon by exploring new relations between the mundane, the mythical, and the universal.

1. A Previously Unknown Physicist Becomes World Famous

Albert Einstein (1879–1955) was a little-known university professor working in Berlin until one day everything changed for him. He was catapulted to fame on November 7, 1919, when a solar eclipse proved his general theory of relativity—a contribution that continues to be one of the most successful discoveries of all time, one that has been confirmed over and over again by numerous experiments. From that day onward he would become a celebrity-scientist: a widely consulted oracle who commented on a dizzying variety of topics, human and non-human. Einstein is still one of the most famous persons in history. He has graced the covers of TIME magazine no less than four times, more than any other scientist so far. His work has stood the test of time just as much as his image. The man and his work are essential to western civilization, both symbolically and practically. Throughout the first three decades of Einstein's life, almost no one, aside from some close supporters, considered him a genius. How and why did this perception change so dramatically almost overnight?

News stories about Einstein appeared on the first Friday of November 1919 and proliferated shortly thereafter. Journalists credited him with revolutionizing not only physics, but also everyday notions of time and space. The first headline of *The Times* of London read "REVOLUTION IN SCIENCE/ NEW THEORY OF THE UNIVERSE/ NEWTONIAN IDEAS OVERTHROWN." The next Saturday the newspaper followed up with "THE REVOLUTION IN SCIENCE/ EINSTEIN v. NEWTON/ VIEWS OF EMINENT PHYSICISTS." Two days later, the *New York Times* received a special cable from London. It joined in the chorus across the Atlantic, reporting "LIGHTS ALL ASKEW IN THE HEAVENS" followed by "Men of Science More or Less Agog Over Results of Eclipse Observations" and "Stars Not Where They Seemed or Were Calculated to be, but Nobody Need Worry."

That day was the first time Einstein made news, but it would not be the last. Most of our general understanding of Einstein was shaped by these early news reports. Since then, biographers have filled many gaps, striving to give us the most complete picture of the man.

Most details of his early life are based on documentary evidence (such as his birth certificate, school and exam records), recollections of those who knew him, and from Einstein himself. Beyond an agreement on the basic facts of his life, portrayals of his character and personality oscillate to extremes. He is sometimes described (as his sister did) as an ambitious and stubborn workhorse, while at other times he is shown to be a lofty dreamer unconcerned with the prosaic (as most biographers consider him). Sometimes, he appears as a fun-loving and flirtatious adventurer who enjoys socializing. Other times, he is described as lonely and dead-serious in his obsessive contemplation of nature. Many readers, ranging from professional psychologists to casual admirers, have analyzed the story of his life to figure out what made Einstein a genius.

History has given us many "Einsteins." Who is the real one? To form a picture of him as one coherent individual, many scholars have tried to uncover what unites the disparate threads of his life. Others, like the French philosopher and essayist Roland Barthes, have given up on the search for unity, settling instead for an essential contradiction. "Einstein embodies the most contradictory dreams," he wrote, "and mythically reconciles the infinite power of man over nature with the 'fatality' of the sacrosanct, which man cannot yet do without."

Two sides of Einstein stand out for being most diametrically opposed: his public and private side. Einstein reportedly called his public persona his "mythical namesake." Reflecting on his own fame and path through life, he once explained to a friend that in cases such as his "the disparity between what you are and what others believe, or at least say about you is far too great."

The split between Einstein's public and private sides poses unique challenges for any biographer—it is difficult to figure out and convey to readers *who* he really was. The text that follows meets such a provocation in a way that distinguishes it from most standard biographies. It includes as part of his life a study of *how* it is that we have come to know him. The physicist's life and work are part of a much larger epic of a universe that permitted the emergence of a certain kind of genius.

Early years

Albert was born in the city of Ulm in Germany on March 14, 1879, to Hermann Einstein and Pauline Koch. His family moved to Munich before the boy turned two. Albert first attended a local Catholic elementary school and later the Luitpold Gymnasium. His sister Maria, known as "Maja," recounted how he was "born of German Israelite parents," and was "only moderately talented precisely because he needed time to mull things over." His abilities as a child, even in math, were unexceptional. "Nothing of his special aptitude for mathematics was noticeable at the time; he wasn't even good at arithmetic in the sense of being quick and accurate, though he was reliable and persevering." Little Albert was obstinate and violent. "At such moments his face would turn completely yellow, the tip of his nose snow-white, and he was no longer in control of himself," she recalled. On one such occasion, the unruly boy, even "grabbed a chair and struck at his teacher." But despite these temper tantrums, he would grow up to be a "happy, outgoing and universally liked young man." According to his sister, he was only exceptional because of his work ethic. "Persistence and tenacity were obviously already part of his character and would become more and more prominent later on," she wrote. He was no doubt brilliant, in her view, but "only persistence that does not rest allows an idea to take shape and be recognized as truly one of genius." Maja traced Albert's patient concentration powers directly to their mother's ability to sew delicate embroideries. "The same trait that helped to keep his mother from tiring of the most tedious and complicated needlework manifested itself in her son first in his play and later in his scientific work." While the mother's creations pictured cute animals, musical instruments, and chubby cherubs, her son would grow up to weave a new and wondrous theory of the universe.

Pauline described her son as joyous and devilish. "When Albert is here," she wrote to a friend, "there is so much laughing, joking, and music-making going on that there is not enough time for anything else ... he looks excellent, he has even grown some more and has developed a gigantic appetite." She remarked how her two kids loved to play. "The boisterousness gets out of hand," she noted, "and I become even more the target of the two imps' jokes." Philipp Frank, a physicist and friend, who took Einstein's vacant professorship chair in Prague, agreed with these general depictions many years later: "Einstein was never a killjoy."

Update

During Einstein's youth, physics was undergoing stark transformations. It desperately needed an update. Atoms and molecules had fascinated researchers throughout the 19th century, but 20th-century scientists were increasingly confronting even smaller particles that traveled through longer networks and distances. Matter and energy, just like atoms and molecules, had been topics of wide interest in previous centuries. Yet the most venerated formulas of traditional physics could not adequately explain how these subjects related to each other. In the early 1900s, some of the brightest researchers became interested in exploring the relation between electricity, light, radiation, and heat. Scientists would now concern themselves with figuring out how they could be transformed into each other. They chose the term "photon" to refer to little packets of light, and "electrons" was the name chosen for little packets of electricity.

A new generation of scientists and engineers honed in on these new fascinating topics and technologies. Promising research topics that had received scant attention during previous centuries started to gain prominence.

An invisible world was now proving to be more and more interesting than the merely visible one. Since the 19th century, scientists had convincingly demonstrated that visible light was a small subset of a much larger set of electromagnetic waves. Most of the waves in the electromagnetic spectrum were invisible to human eyes, yet they could be detected by other means. Short waves, named X-rays, were found to pass through walls and bodies and could be detected using photography. Waves on the longer side of the electromagnetic spectrum (infrared light) showed up as heat. Much longer waves, later called radio waves, were soon discovered to produce magnetizing effects even across long distances when they landed on metals. The entire spectrum was fascinating. Scientists wondered if any of these invisible waves could be used for communication or other commercial purposes.

At the time, Einstein was positioned as the young heir to a rapidly growing electric distribution company called J. *Einstein & Co.* The business was founded by his paternal uncle Jakob and financed in part by his mother's family, the Kochs. Albert's father, Hermann, and his extended family were poised to become industrial magnates after they were hired to do the electric lighting for the famous Oktoberfest in Munich in 1886.

One of Einstein's classmates from that time recalled that Albert knew how dynamos, telephones, and electric illumination networks worked. These skills could prove invaluable for his family business. As he grew older, his desire to understand electromagnetic waves and technologies based on them increased. At age 16, he penned a letter which is now considered to be his first scientific contribution. It was addressed to his maternal uncle Cesar Koch and dealt with "the marvelous experiments of [German physicist Heinrich] Hertz," now known for his discovery of radio waves.

Scientists and engineers had long known that light had certain benefits over sound when used for the purposes of communication. Messages could be sent via lighthouses, flag, and semaphore systems to cover long distances, permitting almost instantaneous means of communicating through space. Those based on sound, such as sirens and foghorns, could be used in poor visibility conditions, yet their reach was limited and signals shifted with the wind. Those sent using electricity and wires, through telegraphic Morse code-based systems, required a costly infrastructure that was difficult to maintain and could be easily sabotaged.

When Einstein was a teenager, setting and running electrical and communication networks was a booming business. The financial future of his family was particularly promising after J. *Einstein & Co* landed another large contract: they were invited to install the electric networks of a city south of Milan. Albert's parents and sister eagerly relocated to Italy to pursue the business opportunity, leaving Einstein behind with relatives so that he could finish his studies. His family's Italian adventure would soon go horribly wrong. Soon after their move, the town's governors learned that the company was secretly negotiating a deal to buy the water rights of the Naviglio river in Pavía to power a hydroelectric plant that would furnish the electricity to the town's network. Albert's family was accused of double-dealing and asked to leave. His sister Maja would never forget that unfortunate and life-altering event: "Not only were the assets of Albert Einstein's mother lost at this time, but significant contributions from relatives as well." The company, which had some 250 employees during its heyday, would soon go bankrupt. It was not the last piece of bad news that Albert and Maja would get from their parents. The two would see their father fail again in another similar venture. Maja recalled how Hermann set off on yet another risky deal, which was "doomed to failure from the start." "Most of the invested capital was lost," she recalled because their father stubbornly refused to adapt to "any lower standing on the social scale."

From student to patent clerk

After the unfortunate events in Italy and the demise of the company, Albert was no longer able to depend on his family for employment. At age 17, he moved to Zurich, Switzerland, to enroll in a mathematics and physics teaching diploma program at the polytechnic. He graduated four years later, in 1900. In order to earn a living from physics, Einstein had to continue his studies. He bolstered his credentials by completing his Ph.D. with a short thesis, "On the Determination of Molecular Dimensions," within a few years.

Even with a Ph.D. in hand, Einstein was unable to get an academic position. His difficulties in the job market were such that he even wondered if he was the victim of some internecine backstabbing from teachers or peers. His father intervened on his behalf, writing a letter to a prominent physicist, but Albert's luck did not change. The young graduate eventually turned to private tutoring to make ends meet, barely earning a living.

After years of struggling, he found more secure yet joyless employment as a second-class clerk at the patent office in the Swiss capital, Bern. Before he had turned 30, he considered his career mostly a failure. In his own words, he was a lowly bureaucrat, a "respectable federal *ink pisser*," who sat at his desk every day analyzing patent applications.

Although the position lacked glamour and prestige, it turned out to be a blessing in disguise for his career. Valuable proprietary information crossed his desk every day, affording him a front-row view of some of the most exciting technological innovations of his era and giving him a particular edge over physicists who were not exposed to the wonderful modern gadgets in development at that time. While academic physicists were trapped in ivory towers teaching their disciplines' most orthodox rules over and over again, Einstein was free to think about physics in an unorthodox and unfettered way.

The first two decades of the 20th century were a period of vast transformations. These years saw the emergence of all sorts of "modern" things not only in science and technology, but also in the arts, including in music, literature, and architecture. These changes relied on new technological innovations, many of which were based on electricity to transform light and sound in new ways.

Urbanites at the fin de siècle noted that their experience of space and time was changing rapidly underfoot. Their sense of speed and inertia, and even matter and energy, appeared to have little in common with those of their ancestors. Photography was one of many other technologies, which, starting in the 19th century and growing exponentially in the 20th, ushered in new relationships between sensorial reality and the material world. Transportation technologies ferried a growing number of passengers who suddenly found themselves hurled at unusual speeds as more and more vehicles crisscrossed the world at ever more dizzying speeds. With the development of telegraphy, people could receive messages almost instantaneously. With the telephone, listeners could hear distant voices in real-time. Table-top gramophones replayed in sounds that had until only recently been transitory. Dynamos and electrical networks illuminated more and more cities; X-rays penetrated walls and bodies revealing inside eerie skeletons and intimate undergarments. New sources of radiating energy (from radium to uranium) gave scientists hope that new sources of energy might soon be found. The new technological world emerging all around Einstein was next to impossible to understand using the formulas of traditional physics.

During the preceding centuries, and all the way back to ancient times, traditional physics was characterized by the discipline of "mechanics." It was primarily used to explain how "mechanical" machines worked, along with those aspects of the universe that resembled these mechanisms. Mechanics was developed in tandem with traditional mathematics, from basic geometry to calculus, which was useful for modeling gears, pulleys, and levers. These tools could also be used to explain many aspects of our solar system, especially those impinging on agriculture as it related to the seasons and on maritime navigation in relation to the position of the stars and the tides. It was an area of science necessary for understanding water wheels, windmills, and clocks, useful for raising palaces, cathedrals, and fortifications, essential for building aqueducts and boats, and for constructing machinery ranging from agricultural reapers to factory looms. It had good aspects and bad ones. It was as necessary for industry as for conquering new territories and waging war. The science of ballistics stood on its foundations.

Traditional physics could explain how much of the universe functioned, yet it proved lacking when applied to many of the new effects which scientists were noticing all around them. It started to be sorely out of date. Prominent writers at the turn of the century began to note that science was in "crisis." They started referring to it as "old," since it had been developed for entirely different purposes in contexts that differed greatly from the world inhabited by citizens of the new century.

The development of these traditional areas of physics, astronomy, and mathematics was associated with the work of great scientific thinkers. The most prominent among them were Euclid in the 3rd century BC, Nicolaus Copernicus in the 15th, Galileo Galilei in the 16th, and Isaac Newton in the 17th. Their names would become reference points against which the merits of Einstein's contributions would be judged.

During his stint at the patent office, Einstein published four papers during 1905 in the prestigious journal *Annalen der Physik* that would retrospectively be considered miraculous. Retrospectively too, the year 1905 became considered such a fecund one for Einstein that scholars eventually came to refer to it as his annus mirabilis or miraculous year. One of the papers he wrote that year turned out to be "what is arguably the most famous scientific paper in history." It was titled "On the Electrodynamics of Moving Bodies" and is most frequently referred to as his Special Theory of Relativity paper. Another one titled "Does the Inertia of a Body Depend Upon Its Energy Content?" contained the very first musings that would lead to science's most famous equation, $E=mc^2$, relating the concept of energy to that of mass and the velocity of light. Two others focused on areas of research that would eventually earn him the Nobel Prize: "On the Motion of Small Particles Suspended in a Stationary Liquid, as Required by the Molecular Kinetic Theory of Heat" (known as his Brownian motion paper) was key to the establishment of statistical mechanics, while "On a Heuristic Viewpoint Concerning the Production and Transformation of Light" (known as his paper on the photoelectric effect) would become central to quantum mechanics. Scholars see in these texts the very beginning of work that he would complete a decade later. But that was not how Einstein's colleagues thought about his articles when they were first published. Only a handful of physicists showed interest in them, but they were prominent enough to motivate Einstein to return to academia as an untenured assistant professor and helped him get invited to professional conferences. Einstein aspired to become much more.

"On the Electrodynamics of Moving Bodies"

Einstein considered his very first paper on the topic of relativity, titled "On the Electrodynamics of Moving Bodies" as the essential piece that would culminate with his General Theory.

Much to Einstein's disappointment, his relativity paper received only scant attention after it first appeared. Within a few years, Einstein switched strategies: he would try to convince his colleagues of the merits of his theory by reference to an experiment now known as the Michelson-Morley experiment, a collaboration between the American physicists Albert A. Michelson and Edward W. Morley to study the effect of Earth's velocity—the speed at which it hurled through space—on light. Today the experiment is portrayed as a paradigmatic example of a "crucial experiment," a label used by scientists and philosophers to describe a test that could single-handedly be used to prove or disprove a hypothesis.

The Michelson-Morley experiment

Just as Einstein's "On the Electrodynamics of Moving Bodies" (1905) is arguably history's most famous scientific paper, so too the Michelson-Morley experiment is possibly the most famous experiment in the history of science. Yet as with the other experimental tests of relativity, scholars now dispute its actual role in Einstein's work. What is more, some argue that no experiment is ever "crucial" because, in practice, scientists usually explain away inconsistent or even contradictory results by making qualified and gradual adjustments to their theories. Almost never do they discard their hypotheses *en bloc*, let alone the entire edifice on which they stand, and certainly not in one fell swoop. Crucial experiments are more of an ideal and a dream for the scientific community than a reality. Ironically, it is for this very reason that they play a central role in science and our understanding of its powers.

The Michelson-Morley experiment preceded Einstein's theory by many decades. The first trials date back to 1881 when Einstein was three years old. The Prussian-born, American-bred Michelson excelled in precision science by pioneering new ways of measuring that could give results that were accurate by many more decimals than previously. His techniques could be used to measure things that were hard to grasp due to their extremely small sizes or immense velocities. He was particularly interested in measuring very fast things, such as the velocity of the Earth and the speed of light, and very small things, such as lightwave frequencies that spanned nanometers. For his work, Michelson would win the Nobel Prize in Physics in 1907.

Michelson's work came from a long 19th-century tradition that considered advances in science as a cumulative and often collective process based on producing ever more accurate measurements and observations. His most famous measuring technique was known as *interferometry*, which had been developed in the 19th century, and which he improved considerably. By comparing the troughs and crests of light wavelengths against each other, Michelson was able to use the undulations in the light waves themselves as tiny rulers.

Usually, things are pushed and carried by the medium which sustains them. Usually, velocities accrue. The enormous circumference of the Earth, which is approximately 24,901 miles at the equator, rotates around its axis every 24 hours. Additionally, as the Earth orbits around the Sun, it covers a yearly distance of 92.96 million miles, moving at an average speed of 66,616 miles every hour. Someone moving along the Equator speeds through space at some 66,616 miles per hour in addition to rotating eastwards at roughly 1,000 miles per hour, plus the speed of their walking gait or that of the vehicle in which they are traveling if in the same direction, or minus if in the opposite one. We do not feel the Earth's velocity because we move along with it on its surface, but it can become apparent if we separate ourselves from it. When sending rockets into space, engineers take advantage of the Earth's motion as an additional hefty push. Yet light appeared to be unaffected by it. To everyone's surprise, the Earth's tremendous velocity had no influence on light waves.

With light, things did not add up. Einstein would soon seize on that fact to revolutionize science.

Try hard as they might, Michelson and his collaborators could not even notice any difference when they shot a light beam East or West or North or South. One explanation that scientists started considering was that light moved in a different way from how other things were known to move. Michelson's results led him and other scientists to the conclusion that the velocity of light was "invariant," that is, that it was independent of the source of its motion. It did not matter if the source from which electromagnetic waves emanated was moving—the waves themselves moved at their same speed, regardless.

Michelson sent rays of light in various directions, bouncing them off with mirrors, and then comparing their velocities on their way back. He did not like what he had discovered. He repeated his experiments many times, hoping either for a different outcome or for a better explanation of his "null" result. He hoped he might be wrong.

Einstein, on the other hand, liked the outcome: he took Michelson's data and interpreted it differently from its author. Michelson was shocked by how the young physicist used his results and never fully accepted such an original interpretation of his own work. Einstein's relationship with Michelson suffered as a result. It was one of the many relationships which became badly strained during Einstein's ascent to fame.

Max Planck, one of Germany's most respected scientists and an early Einstein supporter, explained in his celebrated lectures what scientists had at first expected. He used the actual example that had initially led scientists and engineers to these considerations. Shortly after the discovery of the wireless transmission of electromagnetic signals by Hertz and others, scientists and engineers began using the technology to send time signals across space to coordinate clocks without needing to set every individual clock against a master model, an otherwise laborious and imperfect procedure. Planck began his example by describing how radio waves could be used to coordinate clocks at a distance. "A time signal," he explained, "is sent out from a central station such as the Eiffel Tower by means of wireless telegraphy, as proposed in the projected international time service." Since the Earth was not stationary, this system would have to take into consideration its movement through space. "Those stations which, seen from the central station, lay in the direction of the Earth's motion, will receive the signal later than those lying in the opposite direction, for the former move away from the oncoming light waves and must be overtaken by them, while the latter move to meet the waves," he said.

Scientists expected that the impetus of the Earth should show a slight, but noticeable difference in the time signal. They found none, which led them to conclude that the velocity of light was independent of the source of its motion. Did this mean that they should add an adjustment to the time signal? Or did it imply that they should change the concept of time itself? The latter argument seemed preposterous to most who considered it. It was not so for Einstein; he argued in favor of completely changing our understanding of time and space, not stopping until he succeeded in convincing his peers and the public of that need. The fact that the measurement unit he used was not a solid, like the traditional meter ruler, but was in fact an electromagnetic wave, became one of the most fascinating points of discussion around his experiment and the theory of relativity. Perhaps light-based standards were simply different from traditional measurement standards? Most scientists were led to that conclusion.

The Michelson-Morley experiment was insufficient to prove Einstein's theory. It was not the silver bullet he had hoped for. Einstein needed more evidence. He had to cover more territory. He tried to *generalize* his work to explain more verifiable aspects of the universe. Einstein needed—and craved—a clear victory. He continued to work hard to achieve it. When almost nobody else did, Einstein believed in himself.

Einstein finally gets tenure

After many years of trying to leave his unglamorous patent office job, Einstein succeeded in getting a tenured professorship in Prague, then part of the Austro-Hungarian Empire ruled by the Habsburg monarchy. He found the city intellectually under-stimulating and the drinking water dirty. His salary was good, but teaching was hard. He felt out of place. He did not speak Czech and did not fit in with Prague's German community either. Einstein's professorship was steps down from those in more coveted metropolitan centers such as Vienna, Zurich, or Berlin. The young professor wanted to climb the academic ladder and move somewhere more prestigious. "When Einstein arrived in Prague," wrote his biographer Philipp Frank, "he looked more like an Italian virtuoso than a German professor, and he had, moreover, a Slav wife." Frank was referring to Mileva Marić, who Einstein had married in 1903 after the two met while studying in Zurich, and who was originally from Serbia.

An opportunity arose for him and his family when he received his first invitation to attend the Solvay Conferences, a prestigious yearly gathering of the world's best physicists in Belgium. He was the youngest scientist in the group and was able to hold his weight among the best of the best. Einstein's career prospects continued to improve, slowly but surely. The family—which by then included sons Hans Albert and Eduard—was soon able to move back to Zurich.

Einstein still longed for a higher paycheck, less onerous teaching responsibilities, and more time for his research. He continued to work hard, to pursue his brilliant ideas, and to approach members of his personal and professional network willing to lend him a helping hand. By the end of 1913, he was called to Berlin as a tenured professor, offered a new institute created especially for him to run as he pleased, and asked to join the Prussian Academy of Sciences. He would once again be the youngest member of the group.

The prospects of leading a pleasant and peaceful life in Berlin were soon cut short. WWI broke out in 1914. A Serbian nationalist shot Archduke Franz Ferdinand, heir presumptive to the Austro-Hungarian throne. The German Emperor Kaiser Wilhelm, the scion of the Hapsburg dynasty, responded swiftly and belligerently. Germany allied itself with Austria-Hungary, declaring war first on Russia and then on France.

Einstein hated war and the tide of nationalism rising all around him. The conflict woke up his political consciousness, motivating him to write counter manifestos and opinion pieces on that topic. Towards the end of October 1915, he started writing "My Opinion of the War," one of many strongly-worded statements about nationalism, militarization, and pacifism. Most scientists during those years were admired members of the national intelligentsia who worked for the state in public universities and societies, and who expected to go to war in the interest of their nations. Most of them marched to the drum of their respective national flags and enlisted in the cause. Not Einstein. He began to criticize his birth nation's position on the war, avoiding military service by virtue of having become a Swiss citizen as a young man. While most of his colleagues immediately abandoned their scientific pursuits to fight in the trenches or become useful to their countries in various ways (such as in the area of wireless signaling and sound detectors), Einstein used this time to gather more evidence in favor of his work and to emerge as a public intellectual.

The General Theory of Relativity

Einstein announced the completion of his General Theory of Relativity in the midst of the war. The now-famous text, "The Foundation of the General Theory of Relativity" of March 1916 capped a decade of work. It was a monumental achievement that would completely change how scientists thought about the universe. The theory claimed the universe was a four-dimensional structure where time was another dimension next to the three previously known dimensions of space. In it, light waves warped themselves in the presence of large masses because of an extremely counterintuitive and original reason. The culprit making them bend so was not due to the force of gravity or to anything else that had previously been seen to make them bend on Earth—it was the actual geometry or shape of the universe itself.

The adjective of "General" in the new title "General Theory of

Relativity" distinguished it from the work undertaken a decade earlier. From then on, he would refer to his earlier work as the "special theory." In this new work, Einstein portrayed science as an impartial judge. His now-famous article introduced an impressive hypothesis followed by a series of experimental tests that could be used to prove it. Today, all three experiments have been widely confirmed. They are known as the "three classic tests" of relativity, frequently appearing in physics textbooks.

Once done with the task of generalizing his early relativity work, Einstein felt "contented but kaput." Historian Matthew Stanley noted how "most of his letters that month consists of him taking a victory lap, informing old friends and colleagues of his success." Almost immediately afterwards, the physicist fell sick. His personal life was in shambles.

For three long years after the General Theory of Relativity was published, most scientists did not pay much attention to it. Even the smaller subset of physicists within the larger community of scientists were largely unmoved. Alternative theories explained the same facts. Einstein's closest colleagues simply did not see why they should change their view of the universe. Aside from a handful of his followers, most continued to work in the same way as before, and Einstein remained unknown to the public. He was a well-respected scientist with a comfortable career and a complicated personal life.

2. The Three Classic Tests

The Michelson-Morley experiment had not sufficed to convince his colleagues of the need to adopt his theory. What else could he do? How many other experiments would he need to convince his peers to espouse it? For more than a decade, Einstein accumulated evidence in its favor and was able to add three more pieces of evidence to buttress its momentous claims.

Einstein was influenced by success stories of famous discoveries that had established the prestige of science from the 19th century onwards. He imitated those models, working hard to show how his theory could predict what others could not.

To this day, the value of science is often credited to its predictive powers. This view reached prominence in the 1800s when one stunning discovery—of the planet Neptune—captivated the attention of the public and the popular press. The classic story of Neptune's discovery dated to 1845, when the French astronomer Urbain Le Verrier noticed that certain calculations of the solar system pointed towards the probable existence of a planet that had yet to be observed. His model turned out to be so accurate that when a German astronomer turned his telescope to the part of the sky where Le Verrier believed the planet should be, he was able to observe it. Le Verrier's discovery soon became a paradigmatic example that helped popularize the idea that theoretical science and abstract mathematics could reveal the existence of previously unknown phenomena. This portrayal was mostly due to the astronomer François Arago, known for having announced the invention of photography a few years earlier. Arago grandiosely claimed that Le Verrier had predicted the existence of a new planet "with the tip of his pen." Not everyone believed Arago's retelling of the discovery. Many of those who studied Le Verrier's work carefully started to dissent from this standard narrative. Insiders noted that the planet had already been seen by others (in Britain) and that

Le Verrier simply stole the show (with Arago's help) from other scientists.

Prediction on the sole basis of pencil-and-paper calculations were a high standard for science at that time. Einstein aimed that high.

The possibility of creating predictions from abstract mathematics was only one of science's many virtues. Its champions often turned to another reason to defend it. Science could be used as a method for determining unambiguous truths in the face of debate. Scientific experiments, in this view, could serve as blind judges in bitter duels, as final and fair arbiters of truth in the face of conflict, offering results not swayed by subjective opinion, human interests, or politics. Einstein admired this aspect of science as well, which became popular thanks to Arago.

The model of science as a judge became firmly established during one of the most famous scientific experiments of all time. It pertained to the topic of light. Was light made of waves or particles? Arago orchestrated a kind of duel between two scientists to get at the truth of the matter. One of them was Armand Fizeau, who argued in favor of the "emission theory" of light which considered it as made up of particles. The other one was Léon Foucault, who believed it was wavelike. Arago arranged a carefully planned contest between them in 1850. After observing the results, Foucault argued that his own hypothesis won. As with the case of Le Verrier's discovery of Neptune, not everyone was convinced about who the real winner was. Scientists would continue to investigate cases were light appeared particulate as well as wavelike (today, the consensus is that it is both). Regardless of the outcome or of the finer details around these discoveries and experiments, these 19th-century models of science became the gold standard for the profession for years to come.

The way "The Foundation of the General Theory of Relativity" was written conformed to a particular model of scientific discovery. It began by stating a bold hypothesis that led to observations, often referred to as "predictions," which would count as tests in its favor.

All three "tests" proposed by Einstein had pros and cons when it came to their power to buttress the theory. One produced results that had been known for a long time. It was therefore a retrodiction rather than a prediction, pertaining to a widely known observation that had long puzzled scientists. The other two observations were mostly expected, yet they dealt with phenomena that were hard to ascertain and difficult to repeat. One of them—revealing the bending of starlight—required complicated measurements during rare solar eclipses. It would finally make Einstein and his theory world-famous.

The first of these tests is known as *the advance of the perihelion of Mercury*, a term that refers to the distance of the planet Mercury to the Sun when it is closest to it. Scientists had known since the mid-19th century that if they used the current laws of physics to calculate Mercury's perihelion and compared the result to actual observations, they were off by 43 seconds of arc per century. The difference had bothered astronomers for years. One of the benefits of Einstein's new theory was that it produced results that matched perfectly with preexisting observations. Yet Einstein's explanation of the discrepancy failed to get much attention since it did not reveal anything new, unknown or unexpected. Quite the contrary.

The second test was even less dramatic. It involved measuring changes in the frequency of light waves, that is, in the distance between crests and troughs which, in the case of visible light, give it its particular color. Einstein proposed that light waves would change frequency in the presence of large masses, moving towards the red side of the spectrum (called a redshift) as they moved away from them and towards the blue when closer. Since the mid-19th century, astronomers had surmised that light waves might be subject to effects similar to those already observed with sound waves, where they grow longer as they travel away from the receiving instrument and shorter when going towards it. Why would it be any different for light waves? Additional causes—not only those of waves moving towards or away from us—might produce similar shifts.

The final test was the bending of starlight in the vicinity of a large mass. Large masses created tremendous effects around them, traditionally ascribed to the force of gravity. Could masses affect light? Could they make it bend?

Such curvature was hardly perceptible. Why was Einstein so concerned with a minuscule shift showing light bending? Why would other scientists, including astronomers, care so much about testing this aspect of his theory and direct considerable resources to that end?

Testing Einstein's hypothesis was not easy. One way to test it was to study how starlight was affected by the mass of the Sun. Normally, the stars around the Sun were invisible because of the brightness of sunlight. But when the Sun was covered by the Moon, the stars in almost the same line of sight as the Sun became momentarily visible. An eclipse gave scientists just enough time to snap photographs and compare them with the results predicted theoretically. Those in charge of the project hoped to show that the location of the stars in the sky was off by a very slight amount compared to the location predicted by old theories. They hoped they would appear "shifted" due to the curved path of starlight around the Sun.

The change or "shift" the scientists hoped to detect on the photographic plates was incredibly small, about 1/2500th of the apparent diameter of the Sun (approximately 1/3600 of a degree). Never in the entire history of science had such a small difference received so much attention.

Who knew?

The exact way in which light traveled across space impinged on technological and scientific questions of great importance at the time. With telegraphy, the path of electromagnetic wave transmission naturally followed the path of the wire. What path would it take when no wires were involved? During his years at the office, patents pertaining to wireless telegraphy were particularly sought after and subject to intense litigation as inventors battled over priority claims.

Once researchers discovered that invisible electromagnetic waves could be used to send messages wirelessly, they started to study in greater detail the path these waves took across space. As they progressively increased the distance at which they could transmit messages, they noted that these light waves did not travel in straight lines. Since the Earth curved underneath them, the waves did not exit our atmosphere but wrapped themselves on its surface. This was a stunning and widely-welcomed fact: the possibility that electromagnetic waves could potentially be detected at distant locations in remote corners of the Earth fascinated researchers. Curving waves were perfect for communication on a planet that was not flat.

The idea of curving light waves at first seemed counterintuitive. Since ancient times, lines and rays had been defined by reference to each other. Many of the basic principles of geometry were grounded in such a comparison. When researchers began studying "radio" waves, they chose the term in reference to the Latin word for radius and ray. If rays that had always been represented by straight lines did not travel strictly straight, did the basic principles of geometry need to be rethought and rewritten? What about those of physics? Einstein believed so. What appeared straight to some on a particular path might not be so for others on the outside. Physicists could decide to agree on a particular definition of straight matching perfectly well with our intuitive understanding of the concept in order to rescue traditional concepts of time and space, or they could abandon all these concepts completely.

Communication engineers experimenting with early radio technologies were the first to notice electromagnetic waves wrapping themselves around the globe's surface. A researcher writing in 1901 in the specialized technical journal *London Electrical Review*, noted how they "skim or glide over the surface of the earth until further orders" with the consequence that "the curvature of the earth should not affect transmission, and if sufficiently powerful effects are produced, transmission over any distance should be possible." An electrical engineer from Glasgow explained the following year how "the result of the actual experiment can not agree with the rectilinear propagation of the waves, the curvature of the globe seemingly having no effect, disposes of the straight-line propagation." Readers were shocked to learn that these waves "bend around the curved surface of the earth through many degrees of arc." Another expert telegrapher of that era described how engineers had been pleasantly surprised by this discovery. "It was at first thought that this distance would be limited to within a few hundred miles by the curvature of the earth," until they found out that the electrical "disturbance spread over the whole globe and may be detected at any other part of the surface by a sufficiently sensitive electric wave detector."

Engineers did not know what or why they bent so. But the fact that they "follow the contour of the earth or ocean" was accepted wisdom by 1900. In the years that followed, more and more researchers studied light paths with increasing precision, trying to develop better-sending stations and receiving antennas, working mostly by trial and error. By the first years of the 20th century, they had succeeded in sending and detecting invisible wireless messages across more than 2500 miles.

Dreams come true and persistent nightmares

When Einstein completed his General Theory in 1916, he eagerly wrote to a close friend to tell him how this theory was the fulfillment of his "boldest dreams." Yet not everything went smoothly afterwards. A priority dispute soon surfaced.

The leading German mathematician David Hilbert had come up with the same set of field equations at about the same time as

Einstein. Many scholars have tried to establish exact priority between Hilbert and Einstein. The consensus is that drawing such a division is nearly impossible, as the two collaborated with each other intensively and shared their work back and forth. Hilbert's contributions were superior in terms of mathematics; Einstein's in physics. Einstein was worried. Hilbert responded generously to his colleague's concern, effectively granting Einstein the credit he sought.

Understanding why Einstein reacted differently from Hilbert when it came to claiming priority highlights the physicist's views about the worth of his work. Rarely did mathematicians themselves believe so much in the importance of their own discoveries. Under the most common view of their discipline, mathematics was a tool through which scientists could know the universe. They manipulated symbolic abstractions that corresponded in some ways to concrete and measurable phenomena. In Einstein's opinion, mathematics was much more—it was a reflection of the universe itself. While Hilbert's and Einstein's equations were nearly identical, Einstein went further than his colleague in the manner that he interpreted them. He imbued these results with much greater significance.

Einstein's biggest gamble, and one of the reasons he stood head and shoulders above his peers, pertained to how he conceived of the relation between science, mathematics, and truth.

Standing on the shoulders of giants

Einstein's reaction to Hilbert's work vis-à-vis General Relativity shared similarities with how he responded to two scientists who had been the first pioneers in these new fields of physics. These two men were some of the most respected scientists in Europe, inaugurating work on the topics that became central to Einstein long before he even first heard about them. They first showered attention on the Michelson-Morley experiment and on the problem of Mercury's perihelion, described newly discovered properties of light, electricity, photons, and electrons, wrote new equations for them, and studied and explored the relation between their masses, energies, and inertia.

One of them was the formidable Henri Poincaré, a polymath from France recognized as a mathematical genius from a young age. The other one was Hendrik Lorentz, a prodigy from the Netherlands who became professor of physics at the young age of twenty-four and who discovered the relativity equations which Einstein used. Poincaré and Lorentz formed a formidable team, working on such similar topics that one of their colleagues described the latter simply as "the Dutch Poincaré." Neither thought Michelson's result was wrong—on the contrary, both fully accepted his research and developed brilliant explanations for it. Einstein would become embroiled in bitter priority disputes with them.

Poincaré moved easily between public service roles and fundamental research. He was a sought-after expert on mining, transportation, and telecommunications industries, contributing across applied and theoretical sciences in engineering, mathematics, physics, astronomy, and philosophy. He was an evocative lecturer and a widely-read author. He could not be more different from Einstein. Older and bourgeois, Poincaré moved in the dominant conservative Catholic circles of Paris. He came from an elite family accustomed to occupying top-level appointments in prestigious state institutions. He could count a President of the Republic as one of his cousins.

Einstein read Poincaré's work avidly. While working at the patent office, he organized a small book club with two of his closest friends. They called it the Olympia Akademie. Their reading list included a book called *Science and Hypothesis* by Poincaré. The three discussed it over a simple dinner (which typically consisted of sausage, Gruyère cheese, fruit, a small jar of honey, and tea). One of his friends in the group recalled how the book "profoundly impressed us and kept us breathless for many weeks."

Einstein had more in common with Lorentz. The two were in general agreement about some of the most pressing political controversies of their time and saw eye to eye on issues pertaining to the horrors of war, the politicization, and militarization of science, the fate of German scientists who were boycotted in its aftermath, among other topics. Their relationship, although always cordial, was nonetheless extremely tense at certain moments.

Einstein's first paper on relativity theory mostly fell on deaf ears; Lorentz's work, in contrast, attracted more and more attention. One of the few notes that did mention Einstein's drily included the caveat that it "leads to results which are formally identical with those of Lorentz's theory." The contributions were similar, and Lorentz had arrived at them earlier. At first, Einstein had not even cited Lorentz's work, but after readers remarked on their connection, he began referring to his work on this topic as "the theory of Lorentz and Einstein." Eventually, Einstein clarified where exactly the difference between their two approaches lay.

What exactly did Einstein take from his colleagues, and where did he go beyond them? He was only so happy to stand on the shoulders of giants. He wanted to become one, and for that, he needed to show how his work was better than his competitors, collaborators, and colleagues. His correspondence reveals just how much he admired the scientific heroes that had made history and how carefully he studied them. He longed to be as great as them. He would surpass them all.

The areas of interest that first caught Einstein's attention and to decades of research all focused on the topics which had all been inaugurated by Lorentz and Poincaré, mainly the nature of light, magnetism, and electricity, molecular movement, the principle of relativity, and the relations between mass and energy, as well as acceleration and gravitation. His work was so strikingly similar to theirs, that scientists, scholars, and historians have been fascinated with the relation between the three men. Which discoveries were due to the Frenchman and to the Dutchman? Why is the name

Einstein so widely recognized today, while those of Lorentz and Poincaré are only known to specialists?

When compared to many other brilliant scientists of his generation, including Poincaré and Lorentz, only Einstein deserves full crediting for completely changing our notions of time and space. No one else packaged it as neatly and succinctly as he did, and no one fought as hard as he to convince the public and his colleagues that it was worth changing how we thought about time and space in general. *Only a handful* of scientists were familiar with the bewildering new properties of light waves, electrons, and photons, *only a couple* developed a comprehensive mathematical framework for them, and *none other than Einstein* were willing to draw such dramatic conclusions from their work. And yes, too, no one else embraced the spotlight as much as he did.

A crisis in science

Before the century's end, Poincaré raised alarm about a "crisis of science." The harsh judgment came because some of the results of current research on electrodynamics were so bizarre that they seemed almost impossible to reconcile with the old laws of mechanics. These investigations needed a new name, and for the moment, Poincaré simply gathered them under the label of "new mechanics."

This research showed that certain aspects of time were no longer what they were long thought to be. Most surprisingly, it could dilate according to the velocity of the instrument that measured it. A clock speeding through space would show time going slower than a stationary one; what appeared for an observer in motion as simultaneous would not be so for a stationary one. Similar dilation effects beset measurements of length. Poincaré celebrated Lorentz for having first noted that there "is no conceivable experiment that can lead us to discover" a difference between a clock showing dilation and one that did not, with the additional result that no experiment could help decide on one if one of the clock's time was more accurate than the other.

For Lorentz, it was already clear that the velocity of light was "invariant," remaining unchanged even by something as impressive as the Earth's motion. "It will therefore be impossible to detect an influence of the Earth's motion on any optical experiment, made with a terrestrial source of light," he explained. He drew out the significance of Michelson-Morley's experiment's results for the "new mechanics" based on light's invariant properties where velocities did not add up as before. Michelson, like Poincaré, identified relativity theory mainly with Lorentz's work and his equations, more than with Einstein's controversial interpretation of them. "These [the famous Lorentz transformation equations] contain the gist of the whole relativity theory," he explained.

Years before Einstein even started working on the topic, Poincaré nominated Lorentz for the Nobel Prize. In 1902 he sent a letter to the committee co-signed by some of the most respected scientists of those years. They all credited Lorentz for introducing the concept of time dilation, which showed that measurements of time slowed down depending on how fast a clock was moving. Lorentz had studied what happened to electromagnetic clocks that were moving at relative speeds to each other. He developed the equations central to the theory where the time marked by the first clock, usually noted as T_1, depended on the velocity of a second clock, which marked T_2. The equation was simple enough, but it revealed something shocking: a clock would run more slowly the faster it traveled in space relative to a stationary clock. Poincaré described Lorentz's "ingenious invention of 'reduced time,'" in which "everything happens as if the clock in one place slows down in comparison to the other." He also credited Lorentz with changing our concept of simultaneity. Lorentz's "surprising" discovery explained why "two phenomena occurring in two different places can appear simultaneous even though they are not."

The recommendation of Poincaré and its signatories worked:

Lorentz received the coveted prize and sealed his reputation as one of the best physicists of the era. In the traditional Nobel lecture, where the awardee was expected to explain their work to the public, the Dutchman explained how he had arrived at such counterintuitive conclusions about time. "Fortunately, Nature performs this experiment on a large scale," he wrote. "After all, in its annual journey round the sun the earth travels through space at a speed more than a thousand times greater than that of an express train." One therefore "might expect" a "push," since "you know that in the determination of the velocity of sound in the open air, the effect of the wind makes itself felt. If this is blowing towards the observer, the required quantity will increase with the wind speed, and with the wind in the opposite direction the figure will be reduced by the same amount." Michelson, however, found no such push. Lorentz further explained why no one would ever find one.

The research of Lorentz, Poincaré, and Michelson lay the ground for some of the most important discoveries now associated with Einstein's theory of relativity. Yet *they all missed its most important claim*. Lorentz and Poincaré limited their conclusions to making statements about *clock* time. Unlike Einstein, they did not think they applied to time *in general*. Neither of them wanted to start a revolution in physics. Neither did they want to change everyday notions of time and space. Einstein—in contrast—was ready to bring down the entire system. For the rest of his life, Einstein would work extremely hard to differentiate his work from theirs and to establish his priority with respect to relativity theory.

To understand Einstein's fame in relation to Poincaré and Lorentz, many historians have claimed that the latter must have failed to understand fully all the implications of relativity theory. But their relationship to Einstein and to his work is much more complex. The problem was not that they did not understand the theory; the problem was that they did not want to accept it as being so revolutionary. In fact, Poincaré did not even give to science itself such powers. In his modest view, science was simply a successful tool for understanding nature, and scientists were adept at handling such tools. Scientists could use different tools for different things, choosing the most convenient scientific theory for the task at hand. In this view, science was an effective instrument—one that was neither magical nor mysterious.

The Frenchman's position is typically referred to as "conventionalism." It considered physics and math as a convenient symbolic language through which nature can be known in practical terms. Different mathematics are considered as simply better or worse than others, depending on the task at hand. "Mathematical axioms," according to him, were simply "conventions" or "*definitions in disguise.*"

Poincaré's approach to science took the wind out of many of Einstein's most dramatic claims. Einstein, in contrast, wanted scientists to consider science as much more than just useful.

For years, Einstein continued to worry about Poincaré's views about mathematics and science in general. In Einstein's hands, these discoveries would become more than theories and formulas that explained new properties of electromagnetic waves, electrons, and photons—they were a reflection of the very fabric and shape of the universe. His brilliant and controversial idea that made his contribution completely original and unique relied on a radical redefinition of time. The physicist had come to the stunning realization that all the time variables in Lorentz's equations could be reinterpreted as *time in general* and the spatial ones to *space in general*—if one was willing to give up the traditional concepts of time and space. In his view, Lorentz's concept of "local time" could simply be reinterpreted as "time." "Surprisingly," he wrote, "it turned out that a sufficiently sharpened conception of time was all that was needed." With that new point of view in place, he started to refer separately to "the H. A. Lorentz theory and the principle of relativity."

Einstein noted how highly specialized and technical research impinged on cosmological questions so big that they impacted the sturdy laws of theoretical physics that took centuries and at times millennia to update. He was not *just* concerned with the properties of light, with the nature of electrons and photons, or with new gadgets and patents. Most of his colleagues focused on technical and practical issues; Einstein explained how the significance of these discoveries was much more than just about nuts and bolts. He was not one to stay in his lane. His ambition was to think big. He raised the stakes and began to think about how these laws could be rewritten in a radically different way to develop a new comprehensive theory of the universe. He even went farther than that. He made the very nature of time and space his research topic.

As Einstein received more and more attention, his troubles started to grow. Lorentz was not pleased with seeing his equations interpreted in a way he did not fully endorse. He reacted strongly against the bold claim that old notions of time and space *needed* to be deposed. In response, he let the younger physicist stake out his own path, believing that in the end, his own point of view would prevail. In six lectures delivered in Göttingen (1910), Lorentz accepted that Einstein was right but claimed that he was right too: "Which of the two ways of thinking you would like to join, is a decision that depends entirely on each individual." Poincaré agreed with Lorentz's assessment of the importance of his work on relativity theory vis-à-vis Einstein's contributions. In a report on Lorentz's work written that same year, he repeated some of the same claims he had made earlier when nominating Lorentz for the Nobel Prize nearly a decade earlier. Poincaré explained how, in the case of clocks that traveled at different speeds, Lorentz had shown that it was impossible to claim one as correct and the other one as delayed. It is "impossible to detect anything other than relative velocities of bodies with regard to one another, and we should also renounce the knowledge of their relative velocities with regard to the ether as much as their absolute velocities." He concluded clearly: "This principle must be regarded as rigorous and not only as approximate."

In the years that followed, Lorentz would be even clearer about the benefits and disadvantages of each approach, while showing extreme generosity towards his junior colleague. When Einstein felt stuck and belittled in his university position in Prague, Lorentz offered him an olive branch. If he wanted to move, he could take up a job with him in Utrecht. But Einstein aimed higher. A provincial university in the Netherlands might not be much of an advantage over Prague. He angled for a much better job at the prestigious ETH in Zurich, where he had once been a student. With Lorentz's offer in hand, he decided to keep pursuing the position in Switzerland. The strategy was risky personally and professionally, since, as Einstein explained to a friend, he was dealing with Lorentz someone whom he considered "the greatest man in our field, who is also a personal friend."

Einstein was a risk-taker. He needed all the ammunition he could get if he was going to land the job in Switzerland. Might he approach Poincaré for help? The young physicist had met the Frenchman at the Solvay conferences. Such an opportune encounter made it possible for the junior scientist to approach the senior eminence. His correspondence, however, revealed one problem: Einstein did not like Poincaré and badmouthed him, albeit privately. In a letter to a friend describing their first encounter, he described him as "simply negative in general, and, all his acumen notwithstanding, he showed little grasp of the situation." Asking for his help required quite a constraint. Einstein bit his lip, swallowed his pride, and asked the master for a letter of recommendation. The older man responded generously. He recommended Einstein as "one of the most original thinkers I have ever met," and one who held "a very honourable place among the leading savants of his age." Poincaré went on to describe Einstein's working strategy as a kind of guided guesswork that would eventually result in success. The young physicist's future accomplishments, he wrote, would surely stem from his perseverance and originality: "Since he seeks in all directions one must, on the contrary, expect most of the trails which he pursues to be blind alleys. But one must hope at the same time that one of the directions he has indicated may be the right one, and that is enough."

Einstein got the job he wanted, which permitted him and his family to move from Prague back to Zurich, yet all was not smooth between the two men. The following spring Poincaré went to London to deliver a lecture on relativity. As he had done previously in Göttingen, Poincaré defended the usefulness of "ordinary mechanics." This time, he did not even mention Einstein. "What will be our position with regard to these new conceptions?" he asked. Those who decided to adopt the newer ones were not "constrained to do so," he answered. For them, they were simply "more comfortable, that is all." The position of those who rejected them was equally "legitimate." Poincaré believed that in the long run, most scientists would opt against the new system. He was wrong, but he would not live to see it.

Beyond conventionalism and Poincaré

When Poincaré considered the changes brought about by his and Lorentz's contributions to science through their work on relativity, he noted they could be seen as "analogous" to the Copernican Revolution. Yet it would be the name Einstein—and not Poincaré's—that would often be juxtaposed next to one of the most famous thinkers of Western civilization.

In his writings on relativity, Poincaré explained that if physicists opted to change the traditional manner in which they conceived of time and space, a cataclysm would follow, comparable to that which "befell the system of Ptolemy by the intervention of Copernicus." As he foresaw and delineated the most revolutionary consequences of the "new dynamics" he was developing with Lorentz, he insisted that physicists did not need to choose his new theory and "condemn" the old system "in its entirety." In Poincaré's view, the new way of understanding nature via electrodynamics was not meant to supplant the old, traditional theories based on mechanics. The two could coexist, as one was better for some situations while the other one for others.

Comparisons of Einstein to Copernicus would awe the press and the public. The juxtaposition was generally meant as a compliment. Yet in specialist circles, comparisons with Copernicus cut two ways. Philosophers had long argued that Copernicus's real genius resided in that he offered the world a different conceptual structure, a new worldview, or a new language which was better (in some ways and for some people) than the previous one. Yet they also noted that for most practical purposes it made little difference to adopt Copernicus's system over the previous Ptolemaic model (which still considered Earth at the center of the universe). Depending on what use they were put to, scientists found advantages and disadvantages to both. One rendered certain calculations easier, while others became more complicated. Both theories could be tweaked to account for the same facts of observations.

Many scientists believed that there were many cases where two conceptually different explanations could be used to explain the same facts. Was Einstein simply offering to the world a new hypothesis, a complicated and counterintuitive one to boot, that explained the same facts of observation as other competing theories?

Poincaré's strongest statements about the conflict between the old and the new mechanics was given during a widely anticipated conference at the St. Louis World's Fair. The fair itself was a majestic display of the power of science and technology at the turn of the century and the physicist thrilled his listeners by portraying physics at the cusp of a "profound transformation" He noted how the old laws appeared to be on their deathbed, yet he felt optimistic. "We are assured that the patient will not die and even we can hope that this crisis will be salutary," he stated, recounting how despite the revolutionary implications of the new physics, at the scale of most human affairs it was completely identical to the old physics.

Poincaré's references to the Copernican revolution must have impressed the young Einstein. More than a decade later, he would gladly don the honor of having been responsible for such a revolution.

Despite his differences with Poincaré, Einstein continued to work in the direction sketched out by the elder physicist. One of Poincaré's insights that Einstein would expand on was the idea that there was no master clock that could ever serve as a standard for a single, universal, and therefore absolute notion of time. In work published as early as 1889 Poincaré explained how new research into electromagnetic wave propagation revealed a previously unknown aspect of time where clocks went faster or slower depending on how fast they traveled. He stated: "Of two clocks, we have no right to say that the one goes true, the other wrong; we can only say that it is advantageous to conform to the indications of the first." Einstein's words in his "Foundations of General Relativity," were similar: the clock "goes more slowly than the other, because the former is in motion and the latter at rest." What was true for electromagnetic coordinated clocks in Poincaré's work became, in Einstein's hands, a new law of the universe.

Another of the ideas central to Einstein's General Theory of Relativity first appeared in one of Poincaré's presentations to the Académie des Sciences in Paris almost a month before Einstein sent his famous special relativity paper out for publication. In it ("On the dynamics of the electron" on June 5, 1905), Poincaré pointed out how the new formulas of time and space describing electrodynamic phenomena could be expressed *in more general terms* as the quadratic expression "$x^2 + y^2 + z^2 - t^2$" with "invariant" properties in a "space of four dimensions," where x, y, and z referred to the three dimensions of space (typically corresponding to length, width, and height) and t to time. Einstein's notation was slightly different, expressed by the equation $ds^2 = dx_1^2 + dx_2^2 + dx_3^2 - dx_4^2$ (where x_1 = x, x_2 = y, x_3 = z and x_4 = t). In Poincaré's view, the equation showed how measurements of time (t) were related to those of space (x, y, z); in Einstein's theory, it reflected the actual shape of a four-dimensional universe.

After publishing his first paper on the topic in 1905, Einstein followed through with a decade of perspiration. Even the problem of Mercury's perihelion—one of the three tests proposed by Einstein for his theory—was one of Poincaré's initial insights. In 1909, Poincaré proposed as a possible test for the value of the new theories. He explained how Lorentz's and his own research could be used to explain the well-known discrepancy. It could be a "decisive" argument in favor of the new mechanics because "the way in which it corrects the disparity of the classical theory is good." Many years later, when he concluded his work "The Foundation of the General Theory of Relativity," he closed by returning to this test: "Calculation gives for the planet Mercury a rotation of the orbit of 43" per century, corresponding exactly to astronomical observation (Leverrier); for the astronomers have discovered in the motion of the perihelion of this planet, after allowing for disturbances by other planets, an inexplicable remainder of this magnitude."

Poincaré would not live to see Einstein develop his General Theory of Relativity. In the summer of 1912, the great mathematician died from complications related to prostate surgery. After the Frenchman's death, Einstein continued to worry about the value of his work in relation to that of Poincaré and Lorentz. Lorentz remained as active as ever, and he continued to believe that their approach—which did not call for a radical redefinition of time and space—would win out in the long run.

In three lectures given in Haarlem, Amsterdam in 1913, Lorentz took off his kid gloves. He insisted that the decision as to who was right, Einstein or him, could not be left up to experiment and certainly not to Einstein himself, for that matter. He criticized Einstein's "short and quick" dismissal of the fact that Lorentz's interpretation was also valid. The issues at stake, Lorentz insisted, were epistemological: "The evaluation of these concepts belongs largely to epistemology, and the verdict can also be left to this field." In his own view, which echoed that of the recently deceased Poincaré, scientists were free to choose between the two approaches depending on "the mindset to which one is accustomed, and whether you feel most attracted to one or the other view." In

Lorentz's portrayal, the score was at a stalemate, with Einstein's actual contributions having been key, though minimal. "Einstein simply postulates what we have deduced, with some difficulty and not altogether satisfactorily," he concluded.

Lorentz's judgment echoed the well-known phrase by Goethe that "the greatest art of life, theoretical and worldly, consists in changing the problem into a postulate; by doing this, we gain our end." Yet Einstein clearly did much more. One way his contribution has been frequently characterized is by claiming he eliminated a widespread belief in the "luminiferous ether" a substance with a long history dating back to Newton which was then considered as a material that carried light waves through space.

Some scholars pin the difference between Einstein and Lorentz and Poincaré on a disagreement about the existence of this ether. Yet while the ether had remained useful as a concept into the 19th century, by the last decades its existence as a substance or material had already been widely questioned. Poincaré was among those who did not think about it in that way. The ether by then had become something of a placeholder for the concepts of absolute time and space, which neither Lorentz nor Poincaré wanted to discard.

It was a hard sell. Most well-respected scientists in Europe remained convinced well into the early years of Einstein's rise to fame that it was not *necessary* to adopt Einstein's interpretation and that Poincaré and Lorentz had valid points. In response, Einstein began defending the position advocated by Ernst Mach, a philosopher and scientist he deeply admired. Mach argued that the best scientific theories were the most "economical." Einstein argued that his was exactly what characterized his contributions and made them superior to Lorentz's. But Lorentz and others remained unconvinced.

3. Einstein's Magical Message

It would take more than just writing brilliant technical papers to beat his rivals. Einstein had to focus on his delivery style and learn how to write for general audiences. In years to come, he would become an artful messenger who branched out far beyond the confines of specialized scientific journals. He established new friendships with colleagues, mainly mathematicians and experimental physicists, who could help him and his work grow in more exciting directions. His theory was still a diamond in the rough. He was lucky that a handful of colleagues recognized it as such and set out with him on a long journey to make it, and its author, shine in full glory.

One of the first to believe in Einstein and to promote his work at a key moment in his career was Hermann Minkowski, a Polish-born Jewish mathematician who had been Einstein's professor in the Zurich polytechnic. Minkowski formalized Einstein's physical problems as multidimensional. Later on, Marcel Grossmann, a classmate from his Ph.D. days who would generously share his class notes with Einstein, developed the curving differential equations used in General Relativity.

Inventing spacetime

Minkowski's contributions to relativity theory are widely recognized today. In a now-famous lecture delivered in Cologne, Germany, in September 1908, the mathematician trumpeted the accomplishments of his ex-student, articulating their importance in grandiose and poetic terms: "The views of space and time which I wish to lay before you have sprung from the soil of experimental physics, and therein lies their strength. They are radical. Henceforth, space by itself, and time by itself, are doomed to fade away into mere shadows, and only a kind of union of the two will preserve an independent reality." Minkowski explained how this astounding realization was "first discovered by Lorentz, and further developed by Einstein."

Within a few years, Minkowski focused more on Einstein's particular contributions, helping him differentiate his work from Lorentz's and stake out a path that expanded his theory to bear on time and space *in general*. The evocative lecturer argued that relativity was not an artificially constructed hypothesis that could be chosen out of many others, but one that necessarily followed from the new conception of time. He congratulated his colleague for having shown that time had been finally "deposed from its high seat," brought down from the lofty peak of idealistic philosophy to the practical down-to-earth territory of physics. "Our belief in the objective meaning of simultaneity," he argued, as well as that of absolute time, had to be forever "discarded" once the physicist successfully "banished this dogma from our minds."

Apostles of the new gospel

Another supporter soon appeared in France. The physicist Paul Langevin dedicated so much of his time and effort to promoting relativity theory that he become known as the "apostle of the new gospel." Einstein was close to Langevin and admired him deeply. After Langevin died in 1946, he claimed that "it seems to me certain that he would have developed the special theory of relativity if it had not been done already." Langevin raised awareness of Einstein's work by speaking about it in evocative, fantastical, and general ways to broader audiences. Thanks to him, a wide range of intellectuals beyond the narrow community of physicists and mathematicians, ranging from biologists and psychologists to philosophers, started to pay attention.

Langevin was one of the most respected French physicists. He had been chosen to represent France alongside Poincaré at the Congress for Arts and Sciences at the St. Louis World's Fair in September 1904. He had also been a doctoral student of Pierre Curie, and would later fall in love with his advisor's widow, Marie Curie. Years later, his affiliation with the French Communist Party raised eyebrows in conservative circles.

Langevin was instrumental in propelling Einstein to great success by arguing that his theory was "more than a discovery"; it was, rather, "a change of point of view comparable only to that introduced by Copernicus when he put the Earth in its place in the system of the world." The association of Einstein's revolution to Copernicus's would prove long-lasting.

Langevin presented Einstein's work through a colorful example illustrating one of its most bizarre and counterintuitive implications, now known as the "twin paradox" which remains legendary to this day. In a well-attended philosophy conference in Bologna, Italy, in 1911, Langevin referenced the work of Jules Verne, the famous author of *Around the World in Eighty Days* and other fantastical novels. He asked his audience to imagine what would happen if the traveling clocks in relativity theory that ran at different rates with respect to each other, depending on how fast they moved, were replaced with flesh-and-blood human travelers. Would the time of the latter shrink as did the former? Would those humans age less quickly than their peers? Affirmative, answered Langevin, confidently. A voyager on a spaceship who traveled close to the speed of light would age less than humans who remained on Earth. At that time, the scenario of having travelers transport themselves close to the speed of light was completely hypothetical, yet it helped scientists bring attention to the new theory by exploring its full consequences. That possibility led a wide range of intellectuals to consider the repercussions of Einstein's work for their own disciplines. Thanks to Langevin, relativity became much more than a theory of physics; it became an adventure in time travel.

Langevin asked those seating in the audience who among them

would want to "dedicate two years of his life to find out what Earth would look like in two hundred years." All that a willing volunteer needed to do, he continued, was to travel to outer space at a speed close to that of light. Easy, right? The lecturer delivered this question not as a peddler of dreams and fantasies, but as a serious physicist. If someone did indeed agree to go on such a quick trip, he argued, they would come back to find out that time on Earth had passed more rapidly. They would see the world two hundred years later. "The most definitely established experimental facts of physics can permit us to affirm that this will be the case," he confidently stated. For those who did not consider time travel exciting enough, Langevin offered something else. He promised his listeners eternal youth: "One could now say," he claimed, "that it is enough for us to get agitated, to become accelerated, in order to age less rapidly." When Einstein learned about Langevin's presentation, he at first considered it "the thing at its funniest." Soon afterward, he started considering this possibility seriously and dedicated himself to exploring the repercussions of this aspect of his own work.

During the fall following Langevin's presentation, the Austrian newspaper "Neues Wiener Tagblatt" ran an interview with the physicist Ernst Lecher from the University in Vienna with the headline "A Minute in Danger. A Sensation of Mathematical Science." It explained how relativity got "the blood flowing" in scientific circles because it had shown that time could actually shrink and expand. Referring to Einstein, the professor insisted: "I want to call him the Jules Verne of mathematics—but so that I am not misunderstood—a Jules Verne of incomparable correctness and sharpness in thinking."

The time travel stories that became attached to relativity theory gave it an undeniable boost in terms of the attention the theory garnered. Einstein's biographer and colleague Philipp Frank recalled how:

> In the fall of 1912 I first realized that Einstein's theory of the 'relativity of time' was about to become a world sensation.

> ... Einstein had succeeded in proving that under certain conditions time itself could contract or expand, that it could sometimes pass more rapidly and at other times more slowly. This idea changed our entire conception of the relation of man to the universe.

Awing the public was one thing, convincing his colleagues and key members of the intelligentsia was quite another.

Back in France, philosophers called on Langevin as soon as he returned to Paris. They grilled him about his Bologna time travel talk. Their incredulity centered on Langevin's claim that the effects of relativity described by Einstein would also affect biological beings *and* psychological processes and that, therefore, they would affect "the common conception of time." Langevin was bold at first, insisting that the effects on time predicted by relativity theory affect biological processes and beings, assuming that their temporal structure was similar to that of purely mechanical systems. "It is therefore necessary," he explained, "from the point of view of the principle of relativity, that all mechanical, electrical, optical, chemical and biological processes employed for measuring ... time lead to concordant results." Those in attendance were amused but remained largely unconvinced.

Langevin's choice of words was controversial. He described time dilation by saying that "of two clocks, one grows older than the other," arguing that the equivalence between physical and biological processes he described was "very probably" accurate. After hearing some of his colleagues balking at the seamless expansion of the theory from the realm of the physical to the biological, he concluded with the evocative statement, "but we are ourselves clocks."

But wait, are we really just like clocks? Even if one could accept a certain link between clock processes and biological ones, some philosophers insisted that scientists should not forget that humans themselves made clocks in the first place, and that these would simply not exist if humans had not made them: "You are not only one of those clockmakers linked to a clock, you are a maker of clocks," protested one of them. By insisting so, he and other philosophers strove to show that a human component was essential for innovation and discovery, affecting all forms of knowledge, including Einstein's, even when widely considered to be impersonal. Others jumped in, criticizing how Langevin described clocks as "aging" and "growing old." "But so be it! Call it aging, if you want, the acceleration of the hands of a watch," expressed one exasperated member. The physicist Jean Perrin, the leading expert on the theory of Brownian motion, and a strong supporter of Einstein as well as a friend of Langevin's, added with irony: "When physicists say 'aging,' that is one word I especially like." Another philosopher had a brilliant idea to solve the impasse: Why not simply use different terms for what physicists were referring to and for what philosophers meant when discussing time? Why not use "hour" for the time of physics, and "time" for that of philosophy? In this way, they could set boundaries and curb the philosophical pretensions of physicists such as Langevin and Einstein.

After listening attentively to the objections of the philosophers that day, Langevin retreated. He qualified some of the most dramatic conclusions of his Bologna lecture. Modestly, he admitted that he did "not have the pretension of speaking from the point of view of a philosopher." These issues, he explained, were really up to them to sort out: "It is up to the philosophers to say which are the elements of the notion of time that must be modified."

Einstein as a writer

After completing his General Theory of Relativity in 1916, Einstein would dedicate more time to promoting it for general readers. He would try to wordsmith his work into greater acceptance.

To convey its central lessons to a greater public, he began using colorful language and evocative imagery to draw out its full implications. He first tried publishing in some of the few science journals whose editorial policies permitted such flourishes and generalizations. He then completely branched out to write his own book, titled *Über die spezielle und die allgemeine Relativitätstheorie (gemeinverständlich)* (*On the Special and General Theory of Relativity (A Popular Account)*), written with the explicit intention of bringing "someone a few happy hours of suggestive thought." In many respects, the book was typical of the genre.

In some of Einstein's most daring accounts, the traditional concepts of time and space were not only "shadows," as they had been previously called, but also "ghosts." While most of his contemporaries considered them to be real, he argued they were not. "I could never be made to believe in ghosts, so I cannot believe in the gigantic thing of which you speak to me and which you call space." Einstein wrote again about these "ghosts" in an unpublished manuscript, summarizing the main points of his work. "Only ghosts," he argued, would be able to perceive an enormous clock stretched across all of space that would mark absolute time. "There is no audible tick-tock everywhere in the world that could be considered as time," he concluded. Yet if you "ask an intelligent man who is not a scholar" what time is, Einstein continued, you will see that he takes time to be this ghostly concept.

In his popularization book, Einstein explained that some of the concepts in his work, such as the fourth dimension, could elicit fears "not dissimilar to those generated by those ghosts of the theater" by sending "a mystical shiver" down spines. He urged calm, noting that these frightening "theatrical ghosts" could be dispensed with a proper understanding of physics. Yet another creature proved useful for his popular exposition. Einstein asked readers to imagine a strange being who could mess with a person trapped inside a windowless room by attaching a "hook" on the roof outside, knotting it with a "rope" and pulling upwards. Thus held captive and propelled upwards at "fantastical" speeds, readers could see themselves feeling pressure on their legs. Einstein then told them that the push from the floor was practically indistinguishable from that of gravitation, offering proof for his claim that these two forces were identical, resulting from the warping of the universe in the presence of large masses.

Einstein's most successful explanatory image enticed readers by asking them what the universe would look like for a superfast traveler "hastening towards the beam of light" or "riding on ahead of the beam of light"?

In his autobiography, Einstein described how the "kernel" or "germ" of the theory of relativity appeared to him when he first had these thoughts. He explained how the monumental conclusions of his work originated from early childhood imaginings: "After ten years of reflection such a principle [the theory of relativity] resulted from a paradox upon which I had already hit at the age of sixteen" when he first imagined himself propelled through space chasing after a light beam: "If I pursue a beam of light with the velocity c (velocity of light in a vacuum), I should observe such a beam of light as an electromagnetic field at rest though spatially oscillating." He continued to consider this scenario as he grew older, eventually coming to the conclusion that he could find no evidence anywhere in the universe that such an observation would indeed occur. "There seems to be no such thing, however, neither on the basis of experience nor according to Maxwell's equations," he concluded. "The germ of the special relativity theory is already contained in this paradox," he explained.

Most scholars have been led by Einstein's comments from his autobiography to believe that the idea of chasing light waves was his own, yet they were actually common tropes in popular science books of his time. Since he was a young boy, Einstein was fascinated by tomes which he read with "breathless attention" featuring observers chasing light beams. Einstein's favorite author Aaron Bernstein described how, because of the finite nature of the speed of light where faraway events took time to reach our retinas, observers who jumped to far corners of the universe faster than the speed of light could access the past. They could therefore see "the light of the scenes of the French Revolution" or "even farther away, the invasion of the barbarians." Others might move to a different spot in the universe to see how "Alexander the Great is still conquering the world." In his portrayal, observers could pick any moment in history that they wanted to see, since "the representation of Earth's past by way of light will just be advancing into the future, historical events that have long been dead for us will just be coming to life."

Einstein reread these stories, analyzing their scientific basis and their history. In his assessment, these magical reverse-effects could not be seen, because no message, and therefore no traveler, could breach speed-of-light limits. The journalist Alexander Moszkowski recalled a conversation of those years which "destroyed an illusion which had become dear to me. It concerned the fantastic figure, 'Lumen' conceived as an actual human being, imagined as endowed with an extraordinary power of motion and keenness of sight" who, like the others, could jump from star to star at speeds faster than light to see the world in reverse. The name Lumen was given to this creature by the French popular science writer Camille Flammarion.

Lumen and the idea of traveling across the universe alongside light waves had previously attracted the attention of Poincaré. "Flammarion," Poincaré had noted, "once imagined an observer moving away from the Earth at a velocity greater than that of light." What would he see? "For him time would have its sign changed, history would be reversed, and Waterloo would come before Austerlitz."

Einstein studied the provenance of these stories in detail. Flammarion, just as Bernstein, had taken the imagery from yet another source. Moszkowski recalled how the physicist told him that "firstly, Lumen is not due to Flammarion, who has derived him from other sources." The original author was Felix Eberty, who first published pseudonymously. Einstein was so concerned about setting the record straight about how those time stories were scientifically invalid that he would later write a preface to the reedition of Eberty's book. In it, he wrote:

> There is no lack of current interest in this little book, written

by an original, witty person. For it shows, on one hand, a mind that is critically attentive toward the now obsolete concept of time; on the other hand, it shows the peculiar consequences from which the theory of relativity, which so often is being charged precisely for the bizarre nature of its consequences, saves us.

Einstein's immersion in the world of science popularization proved invaluable. By the time WWI ended, he had a series of important successes under his belt: he was widely respected by his peers; he held one of the most prestigious chairs in physics in Europe with a good salary and plenty of time for research; he had authored a comprehensive and original theory of the universe; had written a moderately successful popularization book about it; and managed to place opinion pieces in newspapers about topics far from his field of expertise. But he was not yet the Einstein we know today, remaining largely unknown to the public.

4. Einstein Becomes World Famous

The catalyst came on November 7, 1919, the day one of his recent biographers has aptly titled Einstein's "second birth." News reports that day recounted how a British-led eclipse expedition far off the coast of Africa had proven the strange prediction of a single scientist who claimed that traditional concepts of time and space needed to be completely overhauled. These reports set in motion a process of transformation where Einstein became a symbol of something much larger than himself. The publicity around the expedition changed Einstein's life and the place of science in society forever.

Starlight launched the scientist into stardom. News reports of the eclipse expedition triggered the intense scrutiny which would follow Einstein for the rest of his life. His biographical details, from the crib to the grave and beyond, became endlessly fascinating and fine-combed by thousands of researchers who searched in them for clues of his success. Even the trash at his last residence at 112 Mercer Street in Princeton, New Jersey, was thoroughly examined by the FBI after they grew suspicious of him during the McCarthy era. They too wanted to know who Einstein really was.

But we are jumping forward in time. In 1919, the public was caught by surprise at the mention of a name they had never heard before. They were thrilled to see a dark horse almost no one knew about crossing the finish line victoriously. Astronomers—the paparazzi of the heavens—had caught light doing something unusual at a very special moment. Einstein—a whistleblower from Germany—had told them where they should look and why. Journalists, already used to reporting about the heroic or compromising acts of public figures, were enthralled by this particular assignment involving light.

Only a few months earlier, world leaders had formally gathered together to end WWI. Germany was severely punished for having started the conflict. Yet the drama pertaining to this single scientist from Berlin was of even greater—actually cosmic—proportions. He had loudly and consistently protested the role of his birth country during the war. He suddenly stole the spotlight from the usual cast of heroes and villains. Readers were entertained by stories of a bloodless conflict between a brilliant mind who waged a solo war against deeply entrenched beliefs pertaining to the laws of the universe that had led the scientific community and most mortals astray.

Most early news reports pegged him at 45 or even 50 years old, yet Einstein was barely 40. Prior to the moment when news of his theory broke out, he had worked extremely hard trying to convince his peers of the merits of his work. It had been an uphill struggle.

Einstein was shocked by his sudden transformation into a public figure. So were many others around him, especially his close colleagues and the friends who knew him best. He himself expressed great surprise at his newfound fame in many letters to numerous correspondents: "I have become an idol due to the clamor of the press," he told one of his closest collaborators. "I must serve as a famed bigwig and decoy-bird," he explained to a dear friend. "The role I play," he wrote to another one, "is similar to that of a saint's relics that a cathedral absolutely has to have." Shortly after the widespread news coverage, Einstein noted how in Berlin "every child knows me from photographs." Within a couple of years, the *Frankfurter Zeitung* referred to him as "the most photographed man of the present day."

After Einstein became famous, prominent scientists who were experts on those same topics were taken aback by the public's sense of commotion. "How was it that a mathematical physicist became as popular as a boxer?" asked his colleague and biographer Frank. Others even wrote to the press, demanding it to tone down its hype. Most did not understand what all the fuss was about. But it was too late for caution.

Some of the important cultural changes of the 20th century came to be associated with his name, in one way or another. It rarely mattered if an actual or direct connection to the physicist could be traced—he would become inextricably associated with much that was new in this new epoch. The German newspaper *Berliner Illustrirte Zeitung* was one of the first to tie him to the new dawning era in a general and comprehensive way. "A new epoch in the history of mankind is dawning, and it is inseparably linked with the name Albert Einstein," stated an article. In the span of a few years, he became a point person associated with much that was new in a rapidly changing world.

His sudden ascent to fame was mystifying for him. In one of his letters, he explained how he felt he had become a modern version of the old King Midas, who instead of turning everything he touched into gold, converted it into headline news. "Like the man in the fairy tale, whose touch turned everything into gold, thus it is with me, with everything turning into banner line news," he wrote. Einstein found the hype around him silly. It reminded him of another fairytale. "This business reminds one of the tale of 'The Emperor's New Clothes,'" he wrote to a friend. From that moment onward and for the rest of his life, Einstein talked about how there were two sides to him, a public and a private one.

Einstein eventually decided to embrace the new normal. I will "let myself be shown around like a prize ox," he concluded. He had realized very early in his career that, even in physics, successful contenders played roles much like actors. "If one is pressed into playing one's role as an actor in this farce," he once wrote contemptuously (after his work was criticized by one of his peers), "one is richly compensated for the pain and effort by being able to watch as a spectator the others' playacting." After he became famous, this feeling became more acute. While his public persona grew progressively more mythical and otherworldly, his private life became much the opposite. "Behind the conventional mask of behavior and speech," he would lecture to large audiences, there lay a "real person." In a letter to the famous psychologist Sigmund Freud, he described it simply as "life in the raw."

The announcement of the results of the eclipse expedition of 1919 changed everything for Einstein. Einstein not only gained the ear of the press—he would eventually be consulted by prime ministers, kings, and queens, and would be asked to elaborate on topics far from his area of expertise. Such a clear victory might help him finally take a break from the career and money problems that had long beset him. No longer struggling financially, Einstein first treated himself to a new violin, then a sailboat, and eventually to a summer house in Caputh on the outskirts of Berlin.

The eclipse

Newspaper accounts of the eclipse test hailed Einstein for having predicted that light curved in the presence of large masses. Why was it such groundbreaking news? The way in which astronomers presented the importance of the eclipse measurements could either cause a stir or be quickly forgotten.

One of the first accounts of the expedition was the type of reporting that fell on deaf ears. Although it was written by the leader of the project—the Astronomer Royal Frank Dyson, arguably Britain's most important astronomer at the time—and although it was learned and informative, it failed to captivate non-expert readers. It did not generate a single sensational headline. The importance of the expedition, according to his article, had *nothing* to do with a single man or a single theory. Its purpose was simply "to find out if a ray of light in its passage past the neighbourhood of the sun suffered a deflection in consequence of the sun's gravitation." Dyson did not even mention Einstein's name.

Dyson's sober and technical account would soon be dwarfed by other stories that were written quite differently. They centered on the intriguing figure of a very colorful, rebellious, and quixotic character who single-handedly fought against the status quo in both the natural and political universes. These Einstein-centered narratives soon became serial psychodramas that the public could not put down—much more interesting for readers than the purely scientific stuff. When this man's prediction became the central theme of the expedition's accounts, the virtues of science became clearer for the public: it was a process that could serve as an impartial judge for determining contested truths, winners, and losers. In those portrayals, scientific findings were presented as facts that could not be swayed by opinions, politics, or emotions. At a time of rampant distrust in political, legislative, and juridical authorities, accounts of Einstein's victory gave readers hope that rationality could triumph in a world that seemed to be going mad all around them. Many journalists who reported on the event marveled at how these truths were found "in the midst of war."

Newspapers that hailed Einstein as a winner took their cue from a public presentation at the Royal Society in London the day before. One of the scientists who attended remembered that the meeting was presented as "an intense Greek drama" with "a dramatic quality in the very staging." Organizers that day enveloped one man and his work with an irresistible sense of magic and mystery. Journalists were enthralled.

Articles in *The Times* and *The New York Times* previously laid out the stakes by portraying the eclipse expedition as a test that would determine if Einstein was right. It explained that astronomers had tested for "three possibilities: no shift, the half shift, or the full Einstein shift," where the term "shift" referred to the minuscule change in calculations of the position of the stars in the Sun's vicinity. "The definite establishment of any one of the three as the truth would be an important addition to our knowledge of physics." Another article in *The New York Times* ran with the sub-headline "Test of the Einstein Theory." Why this test was important for physics or for science in general was simply left aside. In accounts such as this, the *why* mattered much less to the public than the *competition* itself and who might win it.

The articles laid the tone for many of the popularization narratives that would follow. Those early popularization accounts explained how Einstein had determined that circles were no longer circular or triangles triangular:

> Put in the most general way it may be described as follows; the Newtonian principles assume that space is invariable, that, for instance, the true angles of a triangle always equal, and must equal, two right angles. But these principles really rest on the observation that the angles of a triangle do equal two right angles, and that a circle is really circular. But there are certain physical facts that seem to throw doubt on the universality of these observations.

The New York Times noted in its reporting how "one of the speakers at the Royal Society's meeting suggested that Euclid was knocked out," explaining that "two lines normally known as parallel do meet eventually, that a circle is not really circular, that the three angles of a triangle do not necessarily make the sum total of two right angles."

Another aspect of the story proved intriguing—its sheer difficulty. *The Times* explained that, although there was no denying the theory was incredibly important, almost no one, not even the scientists involved in the experiments, could explain why. "Even the President of the Royal Society, in stating that they had just listened to 'one of the most momentous, if not the most momentous, pronouncements of human thought,' had to confess that no one had yet succeeded in stating in clear language what the theory of Einstein really was." The fact that understanding the details and the repercussions of Einstein's discovery was nearly impossible for almost everyone became *itself* a reason for fascination. The public was enthralled by the very idea that it could not understand the theory of the genius mind behind it. "A BOOK FOR 12 WISE MEN," noted the subheadline in *The New York Times* reporting on a special cable from Berlin, followed by "No More in All the World Could Comprehend it, Said Einstein When his Daring Publishers Accepted It." It portrayed Einstein as claiming that, despite the revolutionary importance of his theory, "no more than twelve persons in all the world could understand it." Its apparent difficulty became a landmark theme of his work and an often-flaunted virtue.

After publishing sensationalist headlines, *The Times* went into damage control. "Some of the notices in the Press seem to suggest that the ideas we learned at school by aid of Euclid must now be distrusted," wrote one contributor:

> This is altogether wrong, our mathematical ideas of circles, angles, and lines and their properties are right in the same way that 'two and two make four' is right. The recognition of the possibility that when we try to draw circles our compasses suffer the ... contraction and so make, in truth, ellipses—and for aught we know, extremely oblong ones—no more invalidates Euclid than the fact that a blackboard demonstration is made with circles that are by no means round invalidates the teacher's proofs.

But even if not everything was invalidated, the idea that parallel lines could cross was enough cause for concern.

Three weeks later, *The Times* published an account written by Einstein himself. It was introduced with a sober note by the editors, saying:

> It is agreed that the new conception will make little difference to the practical world. Within the range of all ordinary observation, the continuity between the old and the new is infinitesimally close. The laws of physics will become much more complicated, and the laborious work of preparing astronomical tables will become still more laborious. But we may measure our land and believe in our clocks as I we did before EINSTEIN.

It was too late for caution. The "Relativity Craze" had taken off.

The public became enthralled by Einstein's background, described in the press as "a man of liberal tendencies." They zoned-in on his nationality, ethnicity, and revolutionary politics, as well as on his handsome looks and his unambiguous victory. English-speaking readers celebrated him for having protested Germany's role during the war. The first biographical sketch to appear in *The Times* explained how "at the time of the Armistice he signed an appeal in favor of the German revolution," before continuing to describe how he was "an ardent Zionist and keenly interested in the proposed Hebrew University in Jerusalem." In other parts of the world, writers would fixate on his handsome and photogenic looks. A French scientist who became an ardent supporter of relativity marveled at his "very black hair, mixed with silver, undisciplined, curls falling towards the neck and ears, before standing very upright, like an immobile flame of that large forehead."

In Germany, the *Berliner Illustrirte Zeitung* published a front-page photograph of him with the caption: "A new eminence in the history of the world: Albert Einstein, whose researches signify a complete revolution of our understanding of Nature and whose insights equal in importance those of a Copernicus, Kepler, and Newton." The *Berliner Tageblatt* followed up with an account of how the physicist had revealed a "highest truth, beyond Galileo and Newton, beyond Kant" by deciphering "an oracular saying from the depth of the skies."

Reaching bestseller status

After the press coverage he received following the eclipse expedition, Einstein's popular book, which had been published years earlier and was nearly forgotten, suddenly became an instant bestseller. The short book was quickly reprinted and translated into many languages, often appearing with the shortened yet more encompassing title of *Relativity*.

Other talented writers soon joined in to fill in the demand for popular expositions of the notoriously difficult theory, fanning the flames of the relativity craze even further. Some of those accounts remain classics. Pacifists, Jews, Quakers, leftists, and even anarchists were amongst the most enthusiastic riders of the relativity bandwagon. Bertrand Russell, a philosopher, and conscientious objector during WWI who sympathized with many of Einstein's political views, wrote one of the most successful ones. Russell's ABC of Relativity book was so imaginative that his opening scene was narrated from the perspective of a balloonist on drugs who saw a fireworks display during the Fourth of July as a way to introduce the topic of light's finite velocity. Russell visualized the bending of spacetime by describing flies landing on stagnant pools of water who drew the previously flat surface toward them. In other chapters, he vividly described passengers eating at railway carts where "dinner plates which you see as ordinary circular plates, will look to the outsider as if they were oval."

During these years of opportunity, Eddington, who was a pacifist like Einstein, in addition to being a conscientious objector and Quaker, paused his academic research to focus on lecturing and writing for general audiences. In widely popular texts and packed lectures, he jumped on the opportunity to portray to non-scientists science as some sort of magical profession. Scientists noted effects that no one else had imagined, as he described smoking cigars that could last twice as long and indicator dials on aviator's watches going at half speed. In his accounts, Einstein was more than a great physicist—he was more akin to an "exorcist." According to the astronomer, the most important consequence of Einstein's relativity theory was its elimination of the "demon of gravity," that is, its success in disproving the actions of "an intangible agency or demon called gravitation." In its place, Einstein had proposed that the force or pull of gravity was just an after-effect of the shape of the universe itself. "The agent which plays these tricks," in Eddington's retelling, was a "demon." "Einstein has exorcised the demon," he explained to a theater in Oxford, uttering a phrase that he would repeat in various venues for more than a decade.

Paperbacks were followed by films. In the United States, Fleischer Studios, creators of Superman and Betty Boop, produced "The

Einstein Relativity Film." It became one of the most-watched documentaries of that era, with one biographer claiming that "when a film on Einstein was shown at the Museum of Natural History the scene became a riot."

Mass media spurred the myth that Einstein was a solitary genius who rarely interacted with the outside world. Since day one, the daily press had mischaracterized the scientist as someone working "close to the stars he studies, not with a telescope, but rather with the mental eye, and so far only as they come within the range of his mathematical formulae." The film's narrative started with a similar *mise en scene*: "There sits in a quiet little study in Europe a genius." The exigencies of new forms of storytelling connected to new media resulted in short plots that jumped in one giant leap from the brilliant ideas of a solitary genius to the establishment of new truths about the cosmos, obscuring Einstein's long, painstaking and collaborative journey, as well as his close attention to experimental work, his experience with technology as a patent clerk, and his work as a consultant for the military and industry.

The "crucial" experiments that weren't

In addition to furthering the lone genius myth, news coverage often lauded theoretical science as an area of knowledge that leads to new predictions and discoveries. The relation of theory to experiment in Einstein's work was much more complicated than how it was reported.

Scholars and the public alike have long puzzled over why Einstein's hunches and predictions were so accurate. More generally, they have asked how theoretical science and abstract mathematics can lead to knowledge of a practical and concrete nature. Is there something inherently magical in the mathematical calculations of genius minds that can lead to predictions and new discoveries?

Einstein's first authorized biography, *Albert Einstein: A Biographical Portrait* (1930) written under the pseudonym Anton Reiser, claimed that the physicist "does not need more than paper and pen" continuing:

> Frequently, he allows even these to sink to his lap, looks dreamily forward, but continues to reflect with the greatest exactitude on physical laws and mathematical equations. Only in rare cases does he need experiments. Others execute these for him.

This portrayal set the tone for many narratives exploring the relation between theory and experiment in his work and in physics more generally. It stood in stark contrast with how he was described in his first unauthorized biography, *Einstein the Searcher: His Work Explained From Dialogues with Einstein* (in the English translation) by the journalist Alexander Moszkowski: "Einstein himself is fond of experimenting, and has had much success in experimental work." When unable to do experiments himself, "he is obliged to appeal to outside help for certain practical tests." Which version is more accurate?

Einstein's private notebooks show how he actually arrived at his experimental results. In every case, he carefully studied all the preexisting experimental data available to him, often writing to his colleagues to ask them to send him the latest results. His work was a laborious trial-and-error process based on modifying and adjusting his hypotheses in light of many different kinds of evidence, including qualitative ones. Before proposing any theories, he would carefully study what other scientists had done, analyze a host of preexisting experiments and observations, adjust his claims, work backwards from known premises, consider other data, readjust his conjectures, and so on—until he felt confident enough to publish. He then made hard decisions about which results he should publish in academic journals, which ones should be left open for discussion within a close-knit group of scholars, which he should completely withhold from sharing, and which ones could awe the public. It was much messier than the neat procedure he reported publicly. Once in print, his most successful scientific articles presented a much more linear narrative, starting with a hypothesis and ending with "predictions."

As the years went by and he grew older and wiser, Einstein changed the way he presented his results. Increasingly, he would present a hypothesis followed by experimental verification in favor of it, conforming to a strict model of scientific progress. He would also take more credit for himself and find clever ways to distinguish his own contributions from those of his colleagues.

Experiment and theory

By the time Einstein decided his results were ready for the limelight, he was so confident of them that experiments were irrelevant for him. When Einstein missed the first big chance to test his theory when an earlier eclipse test was canceled, he expressed some regret. But not too much. In 1914, he wrote to a friend to say that "I am completely satisfied and no longer doubt the correctness of the whole system, regardless of whether the observation of the solar eclipse will succeed or not. The logic of the thing is too evident." This attitude persisted during the successful eclipse test of 1919. After receiving a telegram informing him that the astronomer Arthur Eddington was going to call the results in his favor, Einstein privately told his colleague Planck that he already expected such an outcome (which Eddington did as well). Einstein explained to Planck how, while the result would not be a surprise to physicists of their ilk, there was still much value in it for others. "You have already said many times that you personally never doubted the result," he wrote, "but it is beneficial, nonetheless, if now this fact is indubitably established for others as well." Einstein's biographer Alexander Moszkowski similarly explained how the result had hardly mattered, personally for him: "To the world generally, they gave the irrefutable confirmation of Einstein's Theory of Gravitation, but not to Einstein himself, whose intuition felt itself so certain that the confirmation was a mere matter of course."

To the historian, it is clear that none of Einstein's observations or "three classic tests" from his General Theory of Relativity were either completely new or unexpected. Results for the redshift experiment were neither counterintuitive nor did not seem to call specifically for Einstein's particular explanation. Many scientists had considered the possibility that the wavelength of starlight and of other celestial objects might shift in similar ways to those of sound waves, depending on whether they were traveling away from or towards the Earth. They speculated that other causes might lead to similar shifts and had already shown that magnets could affect them in this way. If magnetic forces could cause these effects, why would they be immune to those ascribed to gravity? Most scientists who had considered the question had good reasons to believe that the gravitational forces around large masses would also affect these light wave frequencies. The frequency shifts produced by large masses, however, were so small that obtaining precise measurements presented enormous technical difficulties. Yet Einstein was among those who felt very confident that one day an experiment would prove him right. In his publications on the topic, he proposed it as a future and potentially decisive test.

The idea that gravity bent light had also been considered for a long time by eminent scientists. Some of the first investigations of the effect of gravity on light date to the 18th century. Since at that time light was often described as "corpuscular" and made up of tiny particles (as per Isaac Newton), it was natural for scientists to think that gravity would affect these particles too. During the time of the French Revolution, the French scientist Pierre-Simon Laplace speculated that if gravity was strong enough, light would be forever trapped by a gravity source. Most scientists concurred: it appeared highly probable to them that masses or the gravitational pull around them would affect light in some way.

So why did Einstein achieve such an extraordinary success while others who ventured to look into these same problems failed? One benefit of Einstein's explanations was that a single theory could explain all of these three effects comprehensively and in a new way: they would all be due to how space and time were no longer a fixed frame of reference but that they curved in the presence of large masses.

The complicated relation between Einstein's predictions and the experimental confirmation around them should in no way detract from appreciating the physicist's remarkable achievements. Einstein acted boldly, hedging strong bets by simultaneously exploring different hypotheses with different results. He did not always get it right, but when he did, he spoke loudly and confidently about his accomplishments. Getting claims wrong was no doubt risky, but the advantages of getting *some* of them right countered any drawbacks that could come from his missteps.

5. Anti-Semitism and Politics

Einstein's contributions were politicized the moment they went public. As he became more famous, the list of his haters grew. He became an easy target for anti-Semites and for militant nationalists who opposed his internationalism and pacifism. Europe's longstanding problematic relationship with all sorts of ethnic minorities had resulted in the most recent targeting of Jews scapegoated for much of what was wrong at that time. After the Russian revolution of 1917, an influx of Jewish immigrants from Eastern Europe escaping from conflict flamed irrational fears in the West—fears of displaced people, which brought out the worst in their host nations. The horrors of the Holocaust lay years ahead in the future, yet nationalist sentiments were already brewing in Germany in the aftermath of WWI.

Much has been written about Einstein's Jewish identity. For some biographers, it was a defining feature of his life and work; others saw it as irrelevant. In her biography of her brother, Maja remarked her surprise at seeing him become more religious than the other members of his family. "On his own, he observed religious prescriptions in every detail. For example, he ate no pork." According to his friend and biographer Philipp Frank, it was important to distinguish among different types of Jewish culture. Frank described Einstein as an assimilated Swabian Jew from Bavaria in southern Germany, which he contrasted to the rich metropolitan Jews of Berlin:

> The fact that Einstein's ancestors were Jewish made a difference, but not to so large an extent as one might expect. During the period when his parents were growing up, the Jews in these small towns of Swabia did not differ greatly from the rest of the population in their mode and way of life. They no longer clung so firmly to their complicated customs and usages, which rendered difficult the growth of

any intimacy between them and the rest of the population; and with the disintegration of these barriers they tended, to an ever increasing degree, to lose their position as a separate and unique group. The life of the Jews in these districts was not similar to that in Berlin, where there was a class of rich, educated Jews, who themselves developed a specific variant of Berlin culture.

On many occasions, Einstein did not consider his identity as centered on his Jewishness. He declared himself to be *konfessionslos* (without religion) a number of times. When asked to prepare his vita for an award given in 1932, he understood his religious heritage as something that could be pinned on his parents. "I was born, the son of Jewish parents, on 14 March 1979 in Ulm," he wrote.

As Anti-Semitism spread throughout Europe, Einstein's religious identity increasingly became a defining theme in the history of his life and work. During his time in Prague, where he was a German Jewish minority in a foreign country, he became a Zionist, believing that the problems facing Jews would be alleviated the moment they had their own nation to call home.

The summer after the English press hailed Einstein's accomplishments, his work was viciously denounced in a series of anti-Semitic anti-relativity lectures delivered at the Berlin Philharmonic Hall on August 24, 1920. Some of the participants attacked the content of his work and him personally, while outside of the venue others distributed political propaganda. Most members of the intelligentsia jumped to Einstein's defense. "I have constantly experienced," wrote Einstein during that period "great kindness" from "my German colleagues and authorities." But a few of them attacked him and the entire field of science that he represented.

Deutsche Physik

The physicists Johannes Stark and Philipp Lenard were some of his most vocal opponents. Their anger grew far beyond Einstein, reaching to *theoretical* physics more generally, which they contrasted against *experimental* physics. "Whether the culprit is a Jew or not," Stark insisted the work of theoretical physicists was overrated. In the prestigious journal *Nature*, he wrote that "a flood of propaganda for them is started by articles in journals and newspapers, by text-books and by lecture tours, if possible around the world." Stark complained about how Jews had consolidated their power by having acquired "numerous chairs in physics, and above all in theoretical physics" from where they wielded a "dominating influence." He proposed instead that scientists work on *Deutsche Physik*, a national interest-based initiative where scientists would focus exclusively on practical and social applications that would benefit the German people.

Einstein understood very well how he was being portrayed in negative terms based on false stereotypes, noting that many were led to believe that "everything is publicity for Einstein." He went on overdrive in response to these events. Together with a growing number of supporters, he increasingly presented a view of science as an activity that did not vacillate with politics. He also claimed that anyone who opposed his theory did it for purely political reasons and would no longer accept scientific critiques as legitimate: "No men of science," he was reported as replying, "are against my theory." When asked about the opposition, he insisted: "that was purely political." Asked to elaborate more about the specific "political reasons," he answered: "Because I am a Jew."

Einstein on identity

These events led Einstein to identify immodestly and associate himself with Galileo as a figure of persecution. He responded swiftly to his critics by parodying Galileo's *Dialogue Concerning the Two Chief World Systems*, precisely the text that had brought the astronomer into conflict with the Catholic Church. Later, he wrote the Foreword to the republication of this same famous text, claiming that even today "we are by no means so far removed from such a situation" as the one that confronted Galileo when he searched for unbiased truth in the face of the Inquisition. From the time he was young, Einstein saw himself as a misunderstood underdog, snubbed and beleaguered, working against an establishment that was stacked against him.

Even as he represented his heritage proudly, Einstein at times held certain stereotypical views about Jewish people. In a published letter he wrote to a German minister in 1929 on the topic of Anti-Semitism, Einstein described Jewish people as having "a want of solid foundations in the individual which amounts in its extremer forms to moral instability." When he explained to Marie Curie the reasons Anti-Semitism was growing in Germany, he similarly noted that "first, Jews generally play a disproportionately large role in public life compared to their numbers and second, many of them (such as, e.g., I) are pursuing international goals." In response to the question "How I became a Zionist," written for the journal of the Zionist Federation in Germany, he explained it as due to their overrepresentation in cultural spheres: "Jews exert an influence on the intellectual life of the German people altogether out of proportion to their numbers," he wrote. "Jewish influence on the press, literature and science in Germany is very pronounced and obvious to even the casual observer." In his estimation, they also overwhelmingly tended to hold socialist views. "It is no mere chance that the demands of Socialism were for the most part first raised by Jews," he noted. Einstein understood them to be paradoxically over and underprivileged. "Were anyone to form a picture of the Jews solely from the utterances of their enemies," he wrote, "he would have to reach the conclusion that they represent a world power." "At first sight that seems downright absurd; and yet, in my view, there is certain meaning behind it," he concluded.

As Einstein became more involved with Zionism, he grew progressively more aware of the challenges facing the "colonization of Palestine" he had initially hoped for. After first learning about resistance from the local population, Einstein decried their "banditry" and "rioting." "Fields cultivated by day," he noted, "must have armed protection at night against fanatical Arab outlaws." Dreaming about a nation where Arabs and Jews could "live as equals," and where Jews would learn to speak Arabic, he argued against a "narrow nationalism" from either faction. While he advocated unlimited immigration to the region, he did not ultimately believe in the project of creating a Jewish state. Towards the end of his life, he was asked to become president of Israel. By then, his distance from the cause was such that he immediately declined.

In his biography, Frank recalled that even as a young man Einstein felt uncomfortable amongst Prussians. He "sometimes expressed his feeling as follows: 'These cool blond people make me feel uneasy.'" Much of his life was directed towards setting himself and his co-religionaries apart from their countrymen. "Let us live after our own fashion," he told Jewish youths who already looked up to him as a role model, "and not ape dueling and drinking customs which are foreign to our nature."

Adolf Hitler and the rise of Nazism

Amongst those who felt offended by these kinds of anti-German comments was a nefarious prisoner in Munich. He had been arrested for attempting to overthrow the Bavarian government on

November 8 and 9, 1923, during what is now known as the *Beer Hall Putsch*.

His name was Adolf Hitler. Shortly before Hitler was arrested after his coup attempt, he spoke to his supporter and key mentor Dietrich Eckart about Einstein. "The physicist Einstein, whom the Jewish press lets themselves marvel at as a second Kepler, clarifies that he has nothing to do with Germanness." Hitler started his correspondence by parodying the work of astronomers who posited the existence of a previously unseen planet, as Le Verrier had successfully done with Neptune and others had tried to do to explain Mercury's perihelion. "The astronomer," he explained, "observes a group of stars, who knows how long. Suddenly he notices: By thunder!, something is wrong! Normally they should be behaving differently with respect to each other. So there must be some hidden force somewhere that is deflecting them. And he calculates and calculates and correctly calculates a planet that no eye has ever seen which is there, as it turns out one fine day." But according to Hitler, politicians were overlooking the possibility that a similar force was affecting politics and history. "That there could be a secret force somewhere that pushes everything in a certain direction," he continued: "He doesn't think about that. But it is there. Since the beginning of history there she is. You know what her name is. The Jew." The discoverer of this alleged force was sentenced to five years in prison, but was granted early-release after less than a year.

Behind bars, Hitler dictated a book titled *Mein Kampf* and dedicated it to Eckart, with whom he had discussed Einstein. The book argued that the Nazi party he was founding "may count with mathematical certainty on achieving victory some day in the future."

Einstein on others

The anti-Semitism that flared up in the 1920s, the rise of Nazism, and the horrors of the Holocaust led Einstein to have a complicated relationship with Gentiles. After he moved to Princeton in 1933 and beheld these developments from a distance, he reflected on his lifelong preference of working exclusively with his co-religionaries. "It is noteworthy that in this long life," he noted in correspondence with his close friend Michele Besso, "I have exclusively collaborated with Jews."

Einstein's views about minorities or under-represented groups are less clear cut. Scholars have only recently begun to untangle his views about Palestinians, Asians, African Americans, Native Americans, and those suffering from disabilities or mental illness, including his own son. While from one perspective some of Einstein's comments appear to be "racist" or to "reveal 'shocking xenophobia'" (as some have claimed), for the most part, he simply trafficked in common prejudices of his era.

During his trip to Asia, Einstein maintained that "it would be a pity if these Chinese supplant all other races. For the likes of us, the mere thought is unspeakably dreary." It was one of many other generalizations. His opinion of the Japanese was completely opposite. When he did not hold racial stereotypes, cultural ones crept in. Even Americans reportedly appeared to him as uneducated. They, he allegedly told an undercover journalist, could be easily duped into believing anything if "one tells them about something tremendous that will influence all future life, and of a theory that is within the realm of comprehension of only a select group of the very learned, and famous names are mentioned of predecessors who also made discoveries." He spoke from experience, as his fame on the new continent was such that in the 1930s an American millionairess donated $10,000 to Caltech in exchange for meeting him. Einstein had no qualms about biting the hand that fed him. His biographer Philipp Frank recalled him joking about how "the ladies in New York want to have a new style every year this year the fashion is relativity."

Einstein's disdain for philistine Americans along with his thick German accent were not his only obstacle towards assimilation. His principled views on race and social justice stood in the way. "The more I feel an American," he explained, "the more this situation pains me. I can escape the feeling of complicity in it only by speaking out." After becoming a U.S. citizen, Einstein was affronted by the racism encountered by those "of darker complexion." He lamented how the ancestors of "Whites" had "dragged these black people from their homes by force; and in the white man's quest for wealth and an easy life they have been ruthlessly suppressed and exploited," adding that their "sense of equality and human dignity is mainly limited to men of white skins." The prejudices he had encountered as a European Jewish man, he understood, were not even comparable. "Even among these there are prejudices of which I as a Jew am clearly conscious; but they are unimportant in comparison with the attitude of 'Whites' toward their fellow-citizens of darker complexion, particularly toward Negroes." Einstein wanted to dissociate himself from that aspect of his new American life. Because of his position on civil rights and his alleged leftist sympathies, Einstein was placed on the FBI's watch list.

Throughout his life, Einstein consistently feared and disdained the masses as an uneducated, inferior, philistine (a favorite term of his), and boorish mob to be feared. "The intelligence and character of the masses," he wrote as a message in a time capsule, "are incomparably lower than the intelligence and character of the few who produce something valuable for the community." Einstein was in every sense an intellectual elitist who believed that there existed "only a few enlightened people with a lucid mind and style and good taste within a century." Relativity, in his estimation, was a theory that could be accessed by beings who possessed a higher level of mathematical rationality which he contrasted to those who relied on their experiences and lowly common sense. For Einstein, our ability to think mathematically could lead us to discard the limitation of our senses to reach broader conclusions about the real nature of the universe. This ability marked our superiority vis-à-vis inferior beings, including animals. When his younger son, Eduard, once asked him why he was so famous, Einstein replied: "When a blind beetle crawls over the surface of a curved branch, it doesn't notice that the track it has covered is indeed curved," he said. The reason "the universe of these beings is finite and yet has no limits," is because they—blind beetles—simply did not know any better. "I was lucky enough to notice what the beetle didn't notice.

6. Light sees the Light

While it was essential for Einstein to draw on previous models of science in order for his work to gain greater acceptance, the uptake of relativity beyond specialized circles depended on its transformation from a topic that was initially state-of-the-art to nearly conventional. As light waves were sent farther and farther away and electric networks covered greater and greater distances, it became increasingly necessary to take relativistic effects into account. In consequence, the theory of relativity began to seem less counterintuitive as it became more widely used and understood, a trend that has continued to this day.

The first big leap in the use of wireless electromagnetic technologies came during WWI, when investments poured into these innovations paid off handsomely. The war had started with messages sent by wires; it ended with portable radio sets that could even be placed on airplanes and could reach almost halfway around the globe. When the war began, only one radio station had the capacity to send signals from central Europe to North America (the station was located in Nauen, Germany, and could reach Sayville, NY). By its end, Asia and South America were within reach. The technology advanced so much that the U.S. Army Press chose to announce armistice on November 11, 1918, via radio. One year later, the *Berliner Illustrirte Zeitung*, which would later cover Einstein's accomplishments enthusiastically, announced: "We will have to prepare ourselves for the fact that soon the telephone will be one of those things we will be carrying around with us all the time, like our watches, notebooks, handkerchiefs and wallets."

The technological universe around WWI raised the bar on the technical and scientific education required for the adoption, implementation, and maintenance of these telecommunications systems. Understanding dynamos, receivers, coherers, antennas, and more required years of schooling. The gap between the lay public and those versed in science and engineering widened significantly during these years. The public's perception that Einstein's science was nearly impossible to understand, and why it was successfully shrouded in mystery, was in large due to these educational gaps.

Many of the technical as well as popular accounts of relativity that proliferated after WWI used examples involving trains, revolvers, bullets, and light flashes. These were not only pedagogically evocative, but they also aptly described the context where these ideas first arose. The military example of "flash and bang" was frequently used to explain one of the theory's central lessons and would become a widely used trope on a pedagogical treatise on the topic. It involved asking readers to contrast the speed of bullets against that of sound and light by picturing themselves on the battlefield or traveling on a fast vehicle while reacting to being shot or hearing the sound of a blast. The American astronomer William Pickering, one of many authors who used these battlefield examples, asked readers to compare the time of "the sound of a gun being used as a signal on the train" against that of the arrival of the bullet which would reach the observer at a different time. He then asked them to think of this example on a moving train. "Suppose that on a calm day when the train is stationary we fire a gun from the engine," he explained, how would this scenario be different from the case where the train was in motion or "if the gun was at the rear of the train"? The Parisian astronomer Charles Nordmann was most graphic. He explained relativity theory by asking readers to compare the speed of light directly against that of the shell fired by the Krupp-manufactured "Big Bertha" howitzer that had been used during Germany's advance toward Belgium. An author who identified the common "flash and bang" trope in the early explanations of relativity theory explained its effectiveness. Readers who might at first resist its lessons would come around to it with these "carefully graduated series" of battlefield examples: "beginning with the familiar 'flash and bang' of a distant gun, going on to two guns between which he stands, and ending with a full-blown Einstein and trains and light signals."

Relativity theory began to make sense to a growing number of readers who had direct experience with the different velocities of light and sound—mainly through their encounter or work with military signals, explosive flashes, fast vehicles, and actual bullets.

Relativity in Paris

Even as the importance of his work grew, Einstein was not satisfied with legating to the world a purely technical achievement. During those years, he worked hard to show that his theory was not merely a convenient or useful scientific tool—one that could be chosen from among others. Instead, he strove to show that it was the only objective representation of the universe itself. Einstein reconsidered the views of the "acute and profound thinker" in a lecture that was subsequently published as *Geometry and Experience* (1921). It attempted to rebut the "conventionalist" view of mathematics. Under that framework, the non-Euclidean mathematics used in relativity theory described some observational data very well, yet it did not reflect the underlying geometry of the universe itself. Einstein considered those mathematical innovations differently. He claimed that the universe *itself* was non-Euclidean (with a modification by the German mathematician Bernhard Riemann). He tried to show that the question of which geometrical conception was true was "properly speaking a physical question that must be answered by experience, and not a question of a mere convention to be selected on practical grounds."

How could Einstein convince more colleagues, especially those who did not change their opinion on the value of this work because of sensational newspaper reports? Einstein tried his best by traveling to Paris to give a series of widely anticipated lectures. By then, he was so famous that photographers, reporters, and filmmakers awaited him in imposing numbers. His visit was "a sensation that the intellectual snobbery of the capital could not pass up." Intellectuals were not the only ones excited by his presence. Crowds gathered around him and the public at large appeared to be on the verge of an unfettered frenzy. When his train arrived at the Gare du Nord, the scientific celebrity descended on the wrong side of the tracks, so that he could escape surreptitiously from the cameras and the crowds. He made his way through dangerous cables and warning signs before arriving at a tiny door that led to the boulevard de la Chapelle, which, in the afternoon, was as empty as the Sahara Desert. Once safe, Einstein laughed like a child. As an additional precaution, he decided not to tell anyone which hotel he was staying in. In one of the modest accommodations where he stayed while traveling for work, Einstein was pleased to find "one piece of fine soap and a tube of toothpaste" which he kept in order to bring something back home for his wife.

Although Poincaré had been dead for a decade, his memory lived strong in France, revered as a national treasure. Poincaré's name came up at the very beginning of one of Einstein's most challenging lectures at the prestigious Société française de philosophie. The event organizer welcomed the physicist on April 6, 1922, by reminding the audience that the Société "had among its founding members another scientific genius: he was named Henri Poincaré." He then described Einstein as the person who had "accomplished the revolution Poincaré had foreseen." The question-and-answer session that followed was even tougher. The forum was challenging for the physicist linguistically. Einstein's French was mediocre. As a youngster, he despised studying languages and received his lowest grades for French in school. That evening a listener complained how Einstein reportedly pronounced "relativity" with two accents as "rélativité" and mispronounced "equations" as "ékations."

Throughout his Parisian sojourn, Einstein tried to combat the view that his definition of time was a fruitful hypothesis or one convenient explanation that could be chosen out of many other viable interpretations of the same facts. "One can always choose the representation one wants if one believes that it is more comfortable to do so than another one for the task at hand, *but that does not have any objective sense*," he insisted, when he was confronted with that claim.

Debating Henri Bergson

Einstein's response to his critics in France was only partially successful. In the audience he encountered another hurdle to his ascent to glory: the French philosopher Henri Bergson, who was not only arguably the most famous European intellectual in the first half of the 20th century, but was also an expert on the topic of time. Bergson had been thinking about relativity theory for more than a decade after he attended Langevin's presentation in Bologna in 1911, the one that introduced the concept of "twin paradox." Bergson's understanding of time remained at odds with that of Einstein and Langevin.

For the philosopher, time was characterized by the emergence of novelty in the world, which science could only capture in partial ways. "Time is that which is done, and also that which makes everything happen," he stressed. When time appeared as a variable in scientific equations, it could not be revealing anything new that was not already built in a mathematical model. For this reason, Bergson argued that the way most physicists used "time" was perfect for practical and technical purposes, but it was based on a reductive notion of a larger concept.

Bergson confronted Einstein in Paris, causing a commotion in intellectual circles that immediately reverberated far beyond France. While claiming to be "more Einsteinian than Einstein," he argued that the physicist's concept of time was based on unexamined assumptions about the relation of human time to clock time. It was an error, Bergson explained then and later in a book published shortly afterwards, to conflate the two. He argued that clocks were instruments built for humans for the purpose of keeping track of events that *mattered* to them so that it was baseless to define time by reference to them. Some of Bergson's criticisms shared similarities with those of Lorentz (with whom he was in conversation), and those of Poincaré (whose philosophical outlook on science had deeply influenced his). All three believed that a final decision about the merits of Einstein's claims vis-à-vis other interpretations of the relativity equations could not come from physics alone, since some of its assertions were based on unacknowledged philosophical assumptions.

In the philosopher's view, Einstein was not thinking through all the complexities of time. In particular, he was neither considering how the time of the physicists intersected with human time, or how time brought with it the emergence of the new and unforeseeable. He pointed out that the time in Einstein's equations lacked its most essential quality. The confrontation between the two men mirrored a division that would mark the century—that between the science and the humanities, with almost no dialog between disciplines.

The challenge launched by Bergson affected Einstein's standing among many humanists and even some scientists for the rest of the 20th century. In light of Bergson's criticisms, Einstein would never win the Nobel Prize for relativity. When the prize was awarded to him in 1922 (he won it for the year 1921), the president of the committee explained that although "most discussion centers on his theory of relativity" it did not merit the prize since "It will be no secret that the famous philosopher Bergson in Paris has challenged this theory." Bergson, he continued, had shown that relativity "pertains to epistemology" more than to just physics—and so it "has therefore been the subject of lively debate in philosophical circles." Instead, the Nobel was awarded to Einstein "for his services to Theoretical Physics, and especially for his discovery of the law of the photoelectric effect."

Einstein did what he wanted anyway, giving his Nobel lecture on relativity and not on the topic which had earned him the award. He was simply glad to get the Nobel Prize, which he would have given to himself much earlier if he only could, as he explained to the director of the Nobel Institute: "I am very pleased—among other reasons because the reproachful question: Why don't you get the Nobel Prize? can no longer be posed to me. (I reply each time: Because I am not the one who awards the prize.)"

The acrimony between Bergson and Einstein grew with time. In one of the final lectures before his death in 1941, Bergson described the physicist unflatteringly as brilliant, savvy, and ambitious, and markedly different from how the media and the physicist himself promoted his image. According to Bergson, Einstein was driven as much by discipline as by pleasure, becoming a world traveler who "practiced *grand tourism*." And who used political forums *not* for the purpose of promoting relations among scientists and intellectuals, but primarily for his own advantage—to "get in contact with scientists all over the world, corresponding with a princess, lecturing to a queen." Bergson pictured Einstein as an action hero: "I also see him on a ship where the crew conspire to steal and to throw overboard, anticipating them, and drawing his sword to hold back the bandits."

Traveling throughout the world

Einstein would not let his reputation be damaged any further after what had transpired in Paris. Once again, he went on overdrive. After Paris, he promoted his work all over the world and became a global celebrity. During those trips (which included Sri Lanka, Singapore, China, Japan, Palestine, London, Argentina, Uruguay, Brazil, Spain, and many places in the United States) he would often meet prominent members of society and political figures, including archbishops, kings, queens, empresses, and of course, students. When deciding where to go and where to publish, he proved to be a shrewd negotiator of speaking fees and royalties. When an offer from the Imperial University in Peking appeared to him quite skimpy, he asked for more (a thousand dollars), saying that the request was only fair since otherwise "I would be placing other countries too much at a disadvantage that had offered me incomparably greater compensation." South America did not make much of a positive impression on him. An entry in his journal during a trip to Buenos Aires simply read: "Overall impression, lacquered Indians, skeptically cynical without any love of culture, degenerated in ox lard." Argentineans of German descent were a tad worse, as "they seem to be even more nationalistic and anti-Semitic than in Germany proper."

Many of Einstein's trips were dedicated to raising funds for Israel. "Naturally they don't need me for my abilities but because of my name," he told his friend Fritz Haber, an industrial chemist who had reached fame and riches for pioneering the large-scale production of artificial fertilizer and opprobrium for perfecting and producing poison gas. It was his last name's "luster they hope will attract quite a bit of success with the rich kinsmen of Dollar-land," he explained.

During those years, Einstein began to lose hope in collaborative political projects aimed at maintaining the fragile peace in Europe that had been forged after WWI. Once again, he set off on his own path and mission, alienating many of his peers. One particularly difficult and controversial decision he took was abandoning the League of Nations. He had been invited to join as a member of one of its most prestigious branches by Bergson, who was the president of the Committee for Intellectual Cooperation and offered the invitation. To the disappointment of many of his colleagues, including Lorentz (who would succeed Bergson as president), and Marie Curie (also a member), Einstein resigned shortly after joining, then rejoined, then resigned again.

7. Quantum Mechanics and the Atomic Bomb

As political turmoil grew during the interwar period, so did divisions among top physicists. A "good *trick* should not be tried *twice*," Einstein clamored when confronted with a new and bold theory. He was referring to the work of a brilliant colleague, Niels Bohr, who was drawing vast conclusions from quantum mechanics—an exciting and novel field in physics that focused on the tiny subatomic world. Years earlier, Einstein himself had done something very similar to what his most recent rival was now doing. Now that he was senior *and* the most famous scientist in the world, he admonished Bohr, who dared to draw broad implications from research that dealt with the tiniest of the tiny.

Bohr was a prodigy from Denmark who ran his own Institute in Copenhagen and who would receive the Nobel Prize right after Einstein. When Werner Heisenberg, the German physicist who made key contributions to quantum mechanics, compared the two, he claimed that Bohr's influence on the physics and the physicists of the 20th century was "stronger" than anyone else's, even Einstein's.

Bohr gathered around him some of the finest minds of his generation and mentored them in this new field of research. With them, he developed a new way of understanding the universe, which was radically different from Einstein's. To this day quantum mechanics has not been reconciled with relativity theory.

Quantum and relativity physicists debated only interpretations about the universe that could be drawn from certain key examples. Bohr argued that his field of research was fundamental, since everything else in the universe depended on these subatomic constituents; Einstein retorted by saying that Bohr's conclusions and his understanding of these particles were incomplete. None of these physicists had any qualms with the experimental results of quantum mechanics, some of which were easy to reproduce in laboratory settings. Einstein himself made important contributions to the field. His "On a Heuristic Viewpoint Concerning the Production and Transformation of Light" (1905), was retrospectively considered as foundational to the field and led to his Nobel Prize for Physics in 1921. "Owing to these studies by Einstein," noted the presenter of his Nobel Prize award, "the quantum theory has been perfected to a high degree and an extensive literature grew up in this field whereby the extraordinary value of this theory was proved."

One thing was clear: the subatomic world studied by Bohr and the astronomical one studied by Einstein were governed by vastly different laws. Einstein drew most of his conclusions about relativity by focusing on the astronomical expanses of a vast universe. Bohr, in contrast, studied the tiniest elements in nature that were usually cramped inside atoms.

Einstein would spend the rest of his life fighting against the orthodox interpretation of quantum mechanics associated with Bohr (known as the "Copenhagen Interpretation") and searching for an alternative. One of his most respected biographers aptly noted: "The quantum was his demon."

Quantum mechanics was particularly exciting because new research into radioactive elements showed that the inside of the atom appeared to store incredible amounts of untapped energy. The chemist Pierre Curie sounded the alarm about the potentially destructive use of this research as early as 1903, when no one yet had the power to envision the role these technologies would play during WWII when radioactive isotopes were used to create atomic bombs. "It is conceivable that in criminal hands," he warned, "radium can become very dangerous, and one can wonder if humanity has an advantage in knowing the secrets of nature, if it is mature enough to profit from them, or if this knowledge will cause harm." While Pierre Curie was concerned about what would happen if these sources of power fell into the hands of criminals, he was not worried when they were in the hands of his wife. Marie Curie labored away in her laboratory, successfully isolating greater and purer quantities of radioactive substances, unwittingly contaminating herself. As with so many other topics in science, it was Poincaré who took the lead in understanding and communicating the big-picture implications of this research. He stressed the military potential of this research, noting that these subatomic particles could be viewed as incredibly fast "projectiles," while he cautioned that at the state of current research, one "should not count on this artillery to augment the military power of our army."

The potential use of this research for military ends was so evident that many quantum scientists, including Bohr in Denmark and Werner Heisenberg in Germany, would go on to play important roles in researching the feasibility of building nuclear weapons.

Einstein was interested in these strange new elements very early on. In one of his famous *annus mirabilis* papers, he expressed the hope that "perhaps it will be possible to test this theory using bodies whose energy content is variable to a high degree. (e.g. salts of radium)." Although Einstein was never involved in practical work on nuclear weapons, he would emerge as a figurehead for the atomic bomb.

Developing theories to understand radiation and the subatomic world was as exciting as creating new experiments and technologies with them. These particles did not seem to behave like anything previously seen in nature. Physicists had understood atoms to be something like miniature bouncing balls, much smaller but behaving similarly; what lay within the atom, however, was much stranger. Subatomic particles seemed to be in many places at once (an effect scientists referred to as non-locality), they appeared to have different shapes simultaneously, since they were sometimes best described as waves and other times as particles (referred to as wave-particle duality or the complementarity principle), they could not be measured with total precision (referred to as the uncertainty principle), and they could appear or disappear in random and unpredictable ways (a characteristic described as indeterminism).

Young physicists were drawn to Bohr's clever interpretation of these strange particles' behaviors. They began exploring their repercussions across the entire universe and rethinking our understanding of the role of consciousness in it. In Bohr's view, everything in the universe was connected in ways that could not be pinpointed exactly or even absolutely separated, even from ourselves, as it had pockets beyond which nothing could be known with infinite precision, with wavelike and particle qualities, appearing as one or the other depending on what aspect of them was measured. This universe was therefore constantly in flux, changing with us, and affected even by our mere consciousness of it. The technical terms which scientists used to explain these effects were known as non-locality, duality, complementarity, and uncertainty. In combination, they brought about something which bothered Einstein the most: indeterminism.

Schrödinger's Cat and indeterminism

"God does not play dice with the universe," Einstein told Bohr. Bohr, in turn, replied with a sensible request: he asked Einstein to please stop telling God what he could or not do. The two men argued most strongly about the prickly question of determinism. Could everything in the universe be, in principle, known to us? Or did chance intrusions affect it in essentially unpredictable ways?

Those who studied the universe at the level of subatomic particles tended to support Bohr and indeterminism, while those who drew conclusions about the universe from studying its largest masses and fastest known effects, agreed mostly with Einstein. They hoped that science might one day deliver a deterministic understanding of the universe.

As relativity scientists had once done, quantum physicists explored their research's fullest possible repercussions by imagining fantastical scenarios that rivaled those that had been introduced by their relativity peers. One of them was the famous Schrödinger's

Cat, an example born in conversations between Einstein and the brilliant Austrian quantum physicist Erwin Schrödinger.

It referred to an imaginary thought experiment in which a feline was trapped in a box subjected to indeterminate quantum effects (atomic decay) that could kill it by triggering the release of lethal amounts of poison from a flask. The chances of the flask shattering and the cat dying were thus exactly the same ones for radioactive decay. Science dictated that there were exactly equal chances that such an event had actually happened or not. Aside from those probability odds, allies of Bohr's interpretation argued that *nothing else could be known* about the outcome *before* it was actually ascertained. The possibility of decay could only be known probabilistically; The cat's fate could therefore only be known to that same uncertain degree. A 50-50 split in the probability of decay (and therefore cat's death) was there all along, but the outcome of the experiment had to wait until someone actually ascertained it.

To show the absurdity of this interpretation, Einstein argued that the cat had to be simultaneously living and dead before we became aware if he had been spared or killed by the particle that decayed in indeterminate ways. The physically spread-out, half-living, half-dead cat represented, in scientist's lingo, non-locality as well as uncertainty. Schrödinger, who had discovered the famous wave equation governing quantum mechanical systems, explained to Einstein how the "function of the entire system would express this by having in it the living and the dead cat (pardon the expression) mixed or smeared out in equal parts."

Another difference with relativity pertained to the nature of time. In the quantum mechanical view of the world, time was something else entirely. It was unstable, indeterminate, and could be affected by our consciousness of it, by making photons, electrons and other subatomic particles act differently according to how we measured them. "Every look-at-the-clock disturbs the clock's motion in an uncontrollable fashion," Schrödinger posited.

With these examples, Einstein and his interlocutors proved that the world of the really small was as bizarre as that of the spectacularly big. But what was most interesting was that these two worlds could not be more different from each other.

As they had done with relativity, perceptive critics asked how the two worlds were affected by these discoveries and the strange stories that surrounded them. As the subatomic phenomena studied by quantum scientists was made to bear on things at velocities and masses commonly handled at our human scale, its strangeness mostly disappeared and results agreed with those of classical mechanics. In this respect, it was similar to relativity theory, where its effects became mostly negligible when reduced to those perceived by humans.

Yet the places where each *did* impact our social world proved to be of world-historical proportions. More and more electrical networks and electromagnetic waves crisscrossed the globe at planetary scales traveling at the speed of light. An increasing number of subatomic particles and their rays (alpha, beta, gamma) were studied with Geiger counters, cyclotrons, colliders, particle accelerators, and nuclear reactors. Scientists pushed the boundaries of our technological universe as they created new experiments to understand the world at extreme scales. Seemingly esoteric research and the fantastical stories that helped scientists and the public make sense of it impacted the fabric of everyday life. The nuclear era had begun.

Emigrating to America

In 1933 Einstein took up a visiting professorship in Pasadena, California. While he was in the United States, Hitler became chancellor of Germany. Upon returning home to Berlin, Einstein started fearing for his life. He decided to go back to the United States, this time to the East Coast, accepting a professorship at the newly founded Institute for Advanced Study in New Jersey, next to Princeton University. Five years later, the Nazis marched into Vienna. Soon thereafter they annexed the Sudetenland, Czechoslovakia, and Poland. In response to these actions, the Allies declared war on September 3, 1939. The following year, Einstein, who had become the world's most famous refugee, officially became a U.S. citizen.

Einstein's political views changed in light of those world-historical events. He renounced his pacifism and decided to sign a letter warning President Franklin D. Roosevelt of the possibility of building an atomic bomb. The letter which was drafted by close colleagues of his, described the possible production of "large quantities of new radium-like elements" that could produce "vast amounts of power." "A single bomb of this type," it noted, "might very well destroy the whole port together with some of the surrounding territory." It also claimed (erroneously, as it turned out) that Germany had taken "early action" towards building such a weapon.

After learning about the death camps and the mass extermination of Jews during WWII, Einstein swore to never return to his country of birth. He never did. By 1944, Einstein had grown to hate all the Germans, with no exceptions. "The Germans as an entire people are responsible for these mass murders and must be punished as a people," he claimed.

$E=mc^2$ and the atomic bomb

The bomb was not ready to launch by the time Germany surrendered, but war was still raging in Asia. In August 1945, Americans dropped two atomic bombs on the Japanese cities of Hiroshima and Nagasaki.

Einstein's colleagues from Germany followed the news of the atomic bomb explosions while held captive on the outskirts of Cambridge, England. Using hidden microphones, they listened and recorded every word they spoke. The microphones caught Werner Heisenberg, who was in charge of the German nuclear program, tell his colleagues: "I was absolutely convinced of the possibility of our making a uranium engine but I never thought that we would make a bomb," before adding that "at the bottom of my heart I was really glad that it was to be an engine and not a bomb." Scholars have speculated that Heisenberg must have known his captors were listening, and that he spoke those words only to exonerate himself, but what is certain is that the Germans had not come even close to making an atomic bomb.

The "Manhattan project," the American-led secret effort to develop an atomic weapon during WWII, cost billions of dollars and involved hundreds of thousands of staff. Most of the money went towards the vast human resources necessary to build and run large chemical factories for isolating enough explosive material: the right isotopes of uranium, which were extremely rare in nature, and to produce the new element of plutonium.

When the bombs went off, censorship prevented the public and journalists from knowing much about the project and who had worked on it. The government released only one official document, known as the Smyth Report, which explained what these new weapons were and how they had been built. The report focused on a handful of physicists in Los Alamos that had put the bomb together. It brought universal fame to the equation $E=mc^2$.

The painstaking work of the Manhattan Project was so secret that it was even kept out of Congressional oversight. Direct censorship from the military and postwar propaganda affected how the history of the project was told. Physicists rather than chemists, and scientists instead of generals, would be in the headlines. The theoretical physics aspects of the project occupied minimal resources, yet these took an outsized role in the public's imagination.

Extreme simplifications in the official and press reports elided the long chain of shoulders that lay between scientists' initial theoretical speculations and a working bomb. Although Einstein was not involved in any practical work or held any official role in the Manhattan Project, he became a poster boy for the vast initiative, alongside J. Robert Oppenheimer. Within a year, Einstein appeared on the cover of TIME magazine (July 1, 1946) with the equation $E=mc^2$ inscribed on the mushroom cloud behind him. Since then, the association of Einstein's work with the atomic bomb has been central to our "scientific folklore." It was his third TIME magazine cover so far.

The official atomic bomb report claimed that the equation $E=mc^2$ was one of Einstein's most important discoveries. The report stated that Einstein had "concluded that the amount of energy, E, equivalent to a mass, m, was given by the equation $E=mc^2$ where c is the velocity of light." It went on to explain how "if this is stated in actual numbers, its startling character is apparent."

In his 1905 article on the topic, Einstein had merely indicated a possible relation between inertia and energy in words. No such equation had appeared in his publication. For that reason, its discovery had already been subject to debate in Germany among Einstein's enemies.

Einstein's first biographer quoted him as saying that he absolutely did not believe that it would lead to the practical production of near-infinite amounts of energy. Yet from the moment the government's report appeared, the idea that Einstein had been responsible for discovering that mass could be usefully converted into enormous amounts of energy took the public by a storm. According to its author, one kilogram of matter, if converted entirely into energy, would give 25 billion kilowatt-hours of energy, equivalent to all the energy generated by the total electric power industry in the United States for approximately two months.

One prominent journalist writing under the assumed anglicized name of William L. Laurence (née Leid Wolf Seid) convinced thousands of readers of the connection between Einstein, the formula $E=mc^2$, and the bomb. Leslie R. Groves, the General in charge of the Manhattan project, hired him to write articles for The New York Times.

General Groves' hired hand portrayed the theory of relativity as essential for America's victory. "Thousands of young Americans,"

Laurence claimed, "owe their lives to the theory of relativity—which is another way of saying that pure science, no matter how impractical it may appear, pays high dividends in the end." In these accounts, the world's most famous Jewish émigré was also a war hero who fought against the Nazis from the comfort of his office desk. "It is one of the great ironies of history that the German warlords who drove Einstein into exile, were forced to rely on the theory of relativity in their efforts to develop an atomic bomb to save from defeat. The United States, of which Einstein is now an honoured citizen, succeeded where the Nazis failed," he wrote. Laurence's award-winning piece in *The New York Times*, "Atom Bomb Based On Einstein Theory," listed a series of stunning possibilities emanating magically from the "Einstein formula."

> One-third of a gram of water would yield enough heat to turn 1,000 tons of water into steam.
>
> One gram of water would raise a load of a million tons to the top of a mountain six miles high.
>
> A breath of air would operate a powerful airplane continuously for a year.
>
> A handful of snow would heat a large apartment house for a year.
>
> The pasteboard in a small railroad ticket would run a heavy passenger train several times around the world.
>
> A cup of water would supply the power of a great generating station of 100,000-kilowatt capacity for a year.

These colorful essays and the official report on which they were based affected how the public thought about the relation of theoretical and experimental physics more generally. In such accounts, the formula potentially leading to these wonders had emanated magically from a genius brain aided solely with chalk and a blackboard or pen and paper. The public was awed. For his reporting, Laurence was awarded the Pulitzer Prize in 1946. Recently, however, scholars have recognized how the undisclosed conflicts of interest in Laurence's work had affected his narrative and his portrayal of Einstein, leading to calls to rescind his award.

The link between Einstein's research and the atomic bomb was solidified in the public's perception with the appearance of additional articles. One of these included an original contribution by Einstein himself under the label "$E=mc^2$" in *Science Illustrated*. In it, the physicist once again displayed his talent for writing for general audiences and thinking up creative examples. "The atom," he wrote, was "a rich miser who, during his life, gives away no money." "But if every gram of material contains this tremendous energy, why did it go so long unnoticed?" Einstein answered: "It is as though a man who is fabulously rich should never spend or give away a cent; no one could tell how rich he was."

In other contexts, Einstein made it clear that his part in the atomic bomb project "was quite indirect." "I do not consider myself the father of the release of atomic energy," he insisted. But it was too late for subtleties. By then, he was a star hire at the Institute for Advanced Study, which benefited from his prestige even though he rarely attended any lectures. When he showed up at one of them, his student was so surprised that he claimed it was "the only occasion in all my institute years that I saw Einstein present at physics seminar given by someone other than himself."

In the headlines once again, Einstein gave new rounds of interviews, permitted himself to be filmed at his Princeton home, and turned his 70th birthday into a radio occasion for an eager public to tune into. Because some of the historical events in which Einstein had participated took place before new media technologies were invented, Einstein embarked on various reenactments of his own life and work. In 1932, he agreed to redo a version of an earlier lecture so that it could be played on the phonograph. In 1946, he reenacted the one from 1939, when he signed the famous letter to President Roosevelt urging him to support nuclear weapons. By then, Einstein was used to playing Einstein.

8. Skeletons in his Archive

Decades after Einstein's death in 1955, skeletons started appearing in his closet. The biggest one was the revelation that he had had a daughter. The discovery came as a "total surprise" to "all Einstein experts."

Sometime around 1901 Einstein's girlfriend and classmate at the Zurich Polytechnic, Mileva Marić, who would become his wife in 1903, became pregnant and gave birth to a baby named Lieserl. The girl is mentioned a few times in their correspondence. It reveals some initial excitement from Einstein at the prospect of having a child. Yet references to her disappear as suddenly as they enter into their correspondence. To this day, nobody knows for sure what happened to her, and she continues to be a subject of intense fascination and speculation. Some evidence suggests that she was born with a disability or that she became sick with scarlet fever and was given up for adoption somewhere in Serbia, where Marić's family resided. Einstein, who was away during most of the pregnancy and birth, never met the baby. One of his letters asks Marić how the girl was "registered" and if proper "precautions" were taken so that "problems do not arise for her later."

Other revelations pertained to Einstein's infidelities. Throughout his life, Einstein broke many hearts. Of his many romantic relationships and affairs, three women stand out in addition to Mileva: his second wife (and first cousin) Elsa, and Elsa's daughters, Ilse and Margot.

First wife: Mileva Marić

Marić defied stereotypes by moving away from her home in Serbia to study in a male-dominated field of mathematics and physics.

They married in 1903 in a civil ceremony attended by only two friends. Einstein was 24, and she was three years his senior. A year later they would welcome their second child, Hans Albert. Einstein's groundbreaking work of 1905 was done with Marić sitting closely by his side.

Scholars have speculated how much she contributed to Einstein's work. In one letter Einstein referred to the work as "ours," and although the two studied together and conversed about their work—while she did most of the editing late at night—Marić did not contribute much to this work beyond those early years. His relationship with Marić reveals him to have been impetuous and in love during the first years of marriage. However, short years of collaboration and love would soon be followed by decades of anger, blame, and recriminations connected to a long and painful divorce battle.

"I wonder what will last longer: the World War, or our divorce," he once wrote. During this particularly stressful period of his life, one further aggravated by mysterious stomach pains and ill health, Einstein found that the chief source of his problems had most probably come from his choice of spouse. His letters during this bitter period could not be more different from the syrupy ones he wrote as a young lovebird. His mother had always considered Marić to be below them and had opposed Einstein's marriage. "I begot children with a physically and morally inferior person and cannot complain if they turn out accordingly," he wrote to a friend, regretting not having heeded his mother's advice. By then, the only "urgently necessary" solution that he could think of was that physicians "conduct a kind of inquisition for us with the right and duty to castrate without leniency in order to sanitize the future ."

Numerous scholars have noted Einstein's callous and even cruel treatment of his first wife. His closest friends were shocked by how he treated the woman who had given up her career as a physicist and her homeland and family in Serbia to marry him and take care of their children. They stepped in to mediate and to take care of Einstein's two boys. The physicist did not see it that way. Although he was spending most of his time away from his wife and children with his mistress in Berlin, he believed he was making enormous sacrifices for his family. Responding to Marić's letters about the neglect of his paternal duties, he defended himself: "The fact that I am leaving them in your care is a great sacrifice on my part rather than absence of fatherly feelings." After fighting over the terms of their divorce, Einstein moved permanently to Berlin, where he would remarry his cousin Elsa after his divorce from Marić was finalized. Marić, now referred to as the "barbarian," was left behind in Zurich, battling illness and depression.

One silver lining of Marić's years as a divorcée came from her friendship with Marie Curie. Both women were similar in some ways: "foreigners" from Eastern European countries who had married successful scientists. Einstein had initially liked Marie Curie when he first met her, though he eventually grew to find her bitter and cold "like a herring ... her only emotional expression is cursing about things she doesn't like." Curie had been pilloried by the press for having carried out a short affair with Paul Langevin (while he was married and she was widowed), yet, unlike Marić, she emerged out of the shadows of the men in her life to make a name for herself. Marić, in contrast, was never able to pass her Ph.D. exams or to be much more than a sounding board for Einstein's early musings, in addition to being his emotional companion, housekeeper, and editor.

Second wife and cousin: Elsa Einstein

Einstein knew Elsa from the time he was a little boy. The two cousins would play together during family outings. Later in life, he began to appreciate Elsa for her connections in Berlin. As a first cousin, she came from the monied side of the family: her father Rudolf was the brother of Albert's paternal grandfather. Rudolf had lost money in the electrical company belonging to Albert's family, but thanks to his own successful textile manufactory and sales business, he remained wealthy. When Albert once invited his biographer Philipp Frank to dine with them in the middle of the war, he explained how he should have no scruples about the scarcity faced by so many. "My uncle has more food than the per capita average of the population," he told him, "if you eat at his table you are serving the cause of social justice." On her mother's side, Elsa was also related: her mother Fanny was his mother's sister.

Elsa and her immediate family were helpful to Einstein in many ways. Einstein first fell for Elsa's younger sister, Paula, before deciding to pursue the older sibling. He then wrote to Elsa to tell her he was no longer smitten by her sister. "It is hard for me to understand how I could have taken a fancy to her (Paula)," he explained, "But it is in fact simple. She was young, a girl, and complaisant. That was enough." Shortly thereafter, he began having a secret long-distance affair with Elsa.

To Einstein's great delight, Elsa was not shy about using her influences to help him. By 1913, she had orchestrated such excitement about him and his theory in Berlin that various enticing offers came his way: a salaried seat at the Prussian Academy of Sciences, a professorship at the University that did not require much teaching, and the Kaiser Wilhelm Institute, which he could run as he pleased. If he accepted them, the physicist would have to move to Berlin and be closer with her. While still married to Marić, Einstein tried to calm Elsa's jealousy. "I treat my wife as an employee whom I cannot fire," he explained reassuringly, while he also sent his wife a strict set of written rules of behavior so that tensions would not continue to escalate between them: "A. You will see to it (1) that my clothes and linen are kept in order, (2) that I am served three regular meals a day in my room. B. You will renounce all personal relations with me, except when these are required to keep up social appearances." He concluded firmly: "You will expect no affection from me ... You must leave my bedroom or study at once without protesting when I ask you to."

Einstein attributed the professional benefits he received in Berlin in large part to Elsa's efforts. Appreciating the fact that the woman he was sleeping with was pulling the right strings for him, he wrote to thank her: "Your assistance with my appointment has probably not been all that ineffectual," he admitted. Elsa's circle of influence included the controversial and prominent chemist, Fritz Haber. After she introduced Einstein to him, he became an important ally who opened doors for Einstein in Berlin by securing the necessary funding and votes that led to such generous offers. "Haber knows whom he is dealing with," he wrote admiringly to her, since "he knows how to appreciate the influence of a friendly female cousin." Although essential for his everyday life, Elsa's extreme solicitousness annoyed him. "You fidgety filly! Another telegram!" the physicist complained when she would not leave him alone even when he was traveling.

Within a few years, the portly cousin was downgraded from mistress to cuckquean, settling as *valet de chambre* and business associate in charge of arranging Einstein's domestic and professional affairs and collecting fees for autographs and photographs.

Stepdaughters: Ilse and Margot Einstein

Elsa put Ilse, her 20-year-old daughter from a previous marriage, to work as Einstein's secretary. Soon the daughter was on the receiving end of Einstein's advances, which were, reportedly, creeping her out. "I have never wished nor felt the least desire to be close to him physically," she wrote to a friend explaining her difficult situation, proceeding to explain how "he himself even admitted to me once how difficult it is for him to keep himself in check." Ilse went on to say that Einstein was considering her as a romantic partner along with her mother. "He might even prefer me as his wife," she wrote, "since I am young and he could have children with me, which naturally does not apply at all in Mama's case." The alleged plan involved him having a relationship with both women, since Ilse claimed that her stepfather found taboos against love triangles absurd. "A. asserts that these are social prejudices," she wrote. To her confidant, Ilse expressed her dire predicament. "In the end, I would feel like a slave girl who has been sold," she wrote about such an arrangement.

Historians have speculated if Ilse might have had ulterior motives for writing about Einstein's advances, yet evidence suggests that the physicist was indeed smitten by the young woman, and that his behavior with her was neither improbable nor uncharacteristic. When years later he fell in love with Betty Neumann, the young niece of a good friend of his, he asked if she would come to live with him, his wife, and her daughters. After she balked, Einstein responded: "You have more respect for the difficulties of the triangle geometry than I, the old mathematician." Aware that the 20-year difference between them, as well as his marriage to Elsa, posed insurmountable obstacles, he eventually broke up with Betty. "I must let my favorite little toy be taken away from me," he explained to her.

The task of Elsa's younger daughter Margot was to facilitate Einstein's numerous rendezvous and keep them secret from her mother and sister. Margot kept letters with revelations about her stepfather's infidelities. Aware of their sensitive nature, she authorized their release only after the 20th anniversary of her death. She passed away in 1986.

Scholars who have studied Einstein's private life have found in his affairs evidence of his loving side and brutal honesty. They cite his unapologetic raunchiness as a mark of his genius because these trysts show how easily he flaunted social conventions—and of his superior genetics—because of the astounding number of well-documented affairs.

Sons: Hans Albert and Eduard

Einstein's correspondence also gives us glimpses of his relationship with his two sons. His letters sometimes reveal paternal love, excitement, commitment, and patience, but by the time his second child was born in 1904, Einstein was exhausted and frustrated. His relationship with their mother had deteriorated. Acrimony pertaining to divorce and alimony spread quickly to the rest of his family. Einstein first reacted to the news of Marić's second pregnancy by saying that he "was not the least bit angry" but actually happy that Marić would get "a new Lieserl."

The new baby turned out to be a boy whom they named Hans Albert. After Einstein moved from Zurich to Berlin and started spending even more time with his mistress Elsa, he rarely saw his first family. Many in his small social circle probably did not even know they existed. His first-born grew so upset that his father left and how he treated his mother, that at age 12 he stopped answering his letters. His second son, Eduard, born in 1910, was left with almost no memories of the halcyon days when the family had been happy.

Einstein's professional commitments and fame often left his family longing for attention. Once, when the teenager Hans Albert received a letter from his father with an enclosed photograph, he excitedly wrote back: "It is good that photography has been invented these days, since thus at least we get to see you."

The eldest would grow up to be a successful engineer and professor at UC Berkeley, admired by his father as "a fine specimen." Eduard, a talented piano player with "girlish" manners, grew up to hate his father. The animosity was mostly reciprocated, and it intensified after Eduard was diagnosed with schizophrenia and had to be institutionalized for most of his life at the Burghölzli psychiatric hospital in Switzerland. Einstein did not see Eduard for 30 years, throughout which he complained about the cost of his medical care. From afar, he lamented his "wretched condition" and once regretted having him. "If only I had known, he would never have come into this world," he once explained to Hans Albert. To their mother, he was similarly blunt about the fate of these creatures of a lesser God. "One cannot expect one's children that they inherit a mind," he told her.

Both sons remained close to their mother, who cared for Eduard until she died in 1948. Eduard lived until 1965 and Hans Albert until 1973.

Curating Einstein

How did Einstein want to be remembered? He tried very hard to curate a particular image of himself for contemporary and future generations. Numerous sources show how he resisted the claim that he was a publicity hound, an accusation that frequently came from anti-Semitic quarters. He often followed the advice of some of his closest friends on this issue, who were similarly concerned about how much they hurt the physicist's reputation. His concern with such claims is evident in a letter responding to a question by his stepdaughter Margot when she asked him if she could publish a photograph of herself in an article on him. He assented: "The newspaper can print your picture but must not mention your relationship to me along with it." He then concluded with characteristic hyperbole: "Otherwise, my dear fellow countrymen will again say that I am operating an advertising agency in my home."

Einstein was unhappy with most biographies that had been written about him. The first one, based mostly on informal conversations that took place during friendly dinners with the author, worried him so much that he even considered legal action against its author. After realizing that he would most likely lose that fight, he resigned himself to its existence.

The first biography Einstein liked and authorized was written under a pseudonym by Ilse's husband, Rudolf Kayser, whom he affectionately called Rudi. It was published while the physicist was in his early 50s and still living in Berlin. Einstein was not entirely pleased with the outcome, but he was sufficiently satisfied that he let Kayser publish it in languages other than German. He "need[s] to earn money," he explained, and "cannot wait until I'm dead." Einstein considered the book as "accurate," "as good as might be expected," written by "someone who knows me rather intimately" and showing him accordingly "in bedroom slippers." Kayser's account contradicted much of what Einstein's sister, Maja, had said earlier. It recounted how Einstein's high school math work was so impressive that "the talent manifested was that of genius." Little did it matter that none of his teachers thought so. "To the teachers, it was not always pleasing," it explained, "many questions the boy asked embarrassed them to the point of silence."

Most biographies, starting with Kayser's, stressed Einstein's extreme modesty, noted his shabby dress habits, and his lack of concern with mundanity. Recounting how he came to be a physicist, Kayser explained how for him "the choice of a profession, however, had other implications: it made necessary a relationship with society and with a mechanical life constantly controlled by ends-in-view and utilitarian purposes." Einstein allegedly strove for something else entirely: "He was not ambitious: he wanted neither fame nor success." In this portrayal, "his only wish was to be able to lead a secluded, modest, and, at the same time, ethical and intellectual existence." Accounts such as this set the man apart from his context, claiming that he was indifferent to fame and much else around him:

> Einstein is not a "modern" man. Nothing is further from him than a trivial selfishness and particularism of life and interests. No other phenomena are stranger to him than the pursuit of success, the brutality of gain, of lovelessness and of cruelty.

The Einstein described by his colleague, the physicist and philosopher Philipp Frank painted a different picture. "Ascetic instincts were foreign to him," he insisted, noting that "Einstein's conversation was often a combination of inoffensive jokes and penetrating ridicule so that some people could not decide whether to laugh or to feel hurt."

Einstein on himself

There is enough material from Einstein about himself that a recent book about him with the title "Einstein on Einstein" focused intently on autobiographical statements and texts. One of the most comprehensive ones was written when the physicist turned 67. His autobiography, or as he called it, his "autonecrology," would be one of two existing statements from which many biographers have drawn. In his first text, the physicist offered strictures for interpreting identity and action in men of his type more generally. "The essential in the being of a man of my type," he wrote, "lies precisely in what he thinks and how he thinks, not in what he does or suffers." In Einstein's own view, deeds and feelings were secondary aspects of life; thought content and processes were essential. This self-understanding of himself as a *thinker*—not as a doer or sufferer or even less than formed by others' doings and sufferings—fit well with how many others came to understand him: as a producer and container of thoughts. The second one, titled "Autobiographical Sketch," was written about a month before his death in 1955. The two books resembled each other in key ways.

Einstein's portrayal of himself as a thinker more than as a doer affected how the public saw him. In an insightful essay titled "The Brain of Einstein," the essayist Roland Barthes studied how certain iconographic tropes solidified with time:

> Popular imagery faithfully expresses this: *photographs* of Einstein show him standing next to a blackboard covered with mathematical signs of obvious complexity; but *cartoons* of Einstein (the sign that he has become a legend) show

him chalk still in hand, and having just written on an empty blackboard, as if without preparation, the magic formula of the world.

Einstein also portrayed himself as a rebel. He, literally, stuck his tongue out to the media with an image that turned him into such an icon. One of the most ironic aspects of his legacy is how much he liked the now-famous photograph where he appears sticking his tongue out to the world. A recent biographer has uncovered how "Einstein himself was the disseminator of this iconic image: he had many copies made of this photograph and sent it to friends, acquaintances, and colleagues."

Archivist and much more: Helen Dukas

In Einstein's attempts to control his legacy during the last years of his life, another woman played a crucial role. The stunningly good-looking Helen Dukas was Einstein's unmarried secretary from 1928 to his death in 1955. She was an efficient house and gatekeeper, as well as a faithful companion and confidant. Dukas, who was originally from the same town in Germany as Elsa, moved to 112 Mercer Street with the rest of the "harem," as Einstein called his female entourage.

After Elsa and those closest to Einstein died, Dukas was appointed by him as one of two trustees of his estate. The physicist Freeman Dyson, who worked alongside Einstein at the Institute for Advanced Study, remembered the task she fulfilled dutifully: "She fought like a tiger to keep out people who tried to intrude upon Einstein's privacy while he was alive, and she fought like a tiger to preserve the privacy of his more intimate papers after he died." This involved the painstaking work of sifting through Einstein's papers and correspondence. "During the years when Helen ruled over the archive, she kept by her side a wooden box which she called her

"Zettelkästchen"—her little box of snippets." Helen combed through the physicist's archive daily, and whenever "she came across an Einstein quote that she found striking or charming, she typed her own copy of it and put it in the box." Much of the Einstein we know today was the one that "Helen wanted the world to see, the Einstein of legend, the friend of schoolchildren and impoverished students, the gently ironic philosopher, the Einstein without violent feelings and tragic mistakes." Her efforts resulted in the publication of yet another book about him: *Albert Einstein: The Human Side*, containing some of his most famous quotes and statements about love, life, and physics.

Marić's unwritten memoir

The version of Einstein promoted by himself and his female allies succeeded only by suppressing alternative accounts—the most important of which was a memoir by Marić that never saw the light of day.

Einstein was terrified when he learned of his ex-wife's intention to publish her memoirs. He had just written to tell her that she and their sons had been mostly cut off from his will, when he learned about the project. "You did unleash my mirth by threatening with your memoirs." He accused her of being possessed by evil intentions and more:

> Does it not enter your mind at all that no one would care one bit about such scribblings if the man they were about had not, coincidentally, accomplished something special? If someone is a nobody, there is nothing to object to, but one should be truly modest and keep one's trap shut. This is my advice to you. However, if the devil doesn't release his grip on you, write what he demands of you, for heaven's sake. I

have already had to endure so much rubbish about myself from my friends that I will also face yours with serenity.

Einstein concluded by noting that "not only children need a smack now and again, but so do adults, and most especially women." Marić retreated, much to Einstein's relief. He wrote to her again explaining that "what enraged me in your last letter was the threat of memoirs" and how, when he first read the earliest biography about him, "the disgust nearly killed me."

Long after Einstein had died, Marić's ghost came back to haunt him. In 1987, her literary estate was "brought to California by her daughter-in-law Frieda," Hans Albert's first wife. Its contents, mainly consisting of "a secret cache of love letters" were estimated to be worth some 15 million dollars.

The cache included a well-documented manuscript about Marić, written about conversations she had with her firstborn's wife. It contained sensitive information that did not fit well with the image the scientist wanted to bequeath. His allies' efforts to control his legacy were suddenly imperiled. A series of discussions, negotiations, and threats of lawsuits against the Einstein Family Correspondence Trust created by Marić ensued. In the end, the publication proved to be a friendly one after a settlement was reached by all parties. The new contributions to his archive turned out to be a positive addition to our knowledge. In the words of the physicist Freeman Dyson, who helped bring them to the attention of the public, with them, "Einstein emerges as a complete and fully rounded human being, a greater and more astonishing figure than the tame philosopher" which others, and even Einstein himself, tried to curate for posterity.

9. Einstein's Legacy

Einstein died on April 18, 1955. Most of those close to him were already long gone. During the last years of his life, he had been isolated from the physics community, partly for refusing to accept the standard interpretation of quantum mechanics and its consequences for our understanding of the universe. He had failed to complete his own ambitious work, the Unified Field Theory, which he hoped would return physics to the path he considered to be the right one.

Einstein was ready to go. He rejected his doctor's advice to do surgery on his abdominal aorta, which had recently burst for the second time, and which had been the cause of stomach pains during most of his adult life. Doctors had already operated on it once, and he did not want them to try to fix it again. His body was cremated. Ashes were scattered in a nearby river in New Jersey, so as no grave could ever become a monument or a place of pilgrimage. His brain, however, was surreptitiously removed during the autopsy. Only this worthy organ, floating in a jar of formaldehyde, was conserved for further scholarly investigation. Doctors soon noted strange folds in its parietal lobes, which some proceeded to investigate as possibly being essential marks of other genius's brains.

Einstein—living or dead—whole or dismembered—is larger than himself. He was so prominent during his own lifetime, that it seems as if history followed him everywhere. Losing his footing at times, he met an avalanche of significant events, spanning from the Belle Époque to the Cold War, with talent, dedication, wit, and humor—often dark.

Einstein's life reveals much more than the actions of a single man. It offers us panoramic views of some of the most important events of the century, as well as of its changing mores and values. Einstein was well aware of how he came to be associated with almost everything that was new, brilliant, and revolutionary—from

Communism to Cubism. Sometimes he had enough of that. Knowing that some of these associations, especially those pertaining to the arts, had gone too far, he quipped when asked about the alleged connections: it had "nothing in common" with them. Rare moments of resistance did not prevent him from becoming an icon.

Where, then, lay the bounds of Einstein's existence? The search for unity misses what is most distinct about him: how his identity became divided, and the process through which different aspects drifted apart, tells us much about the modern universe that we inhabit. From the year of his birth in 1879 to 1955, when he died, the physicist's life was transformed by the introduction of electric light bulbs and networks, automobiles, airplanes, automatic telephone exchanges, mass-produced items, nuclear reactors and bombs, home appliances, microelectronics, suburbs, highways, and much more. Einstein was young enough to see the very beginnings of this world take root when words such as "electron," "photon" and "neutron" became necessary to understand how many of these technologies worked and were first coined.

Mass media comprised of radio, newspapers, movies, and television marked a world divided into large audiences who received second-hand information about the celebrity scientist and the much smaller community of experts of which he was part. The technological world functioning on the basis of the properties of light and electricity discovered during Einstein's era continues to surround us. His insights are as useful and enlightening as ever. Technologies that nobody could foresee during his time, such as Global Positioning Systems that send signals back and forth from Earth to far off satellites, operate under those same principles, and provide the best verification of Einstein's general theory of relativity, making it the best-tested theory of all time.

Our understanding of the universe changed as the world shifted underfoot. Einstein saw the universe as no one else did because he inhabited a unique place in it. He is therefore an ideal figure through which we can track science in the 20th century and beyond. His contributions not only changed what we know about the universe, but our idea of science changed too. For the most part, science ceased to be considered just a useful tool for manipulating nature, one based on mathematics—a discipline considered little more than a useful aide of concise symbolic descriptions that represent nature. It was also no longer seen as a craft or practice tied to engineering, where advances in our ability to predict and control nature were achieved by gradual improvement and painstaking work. In the new conception, it provided us with an objective and impersonal reflection of the universe itself.

The physicist is a barometer not only for science, but also for the most important founding propositions of modern secular society, where absolute truth, uncontaminated from passion and politics, could be discovered through the appropriate use of reason and experiment instead of through divine revelation. This conception of truth resembled the one it supplanted so much that Einstein ended up considering the scientific profession as being as holy as that of the religious believers of past eras. "In this materialistic age of ours," he wrote, "the serious scientific workers are the only profoundly religious people." Thousands of practitioners, young or old, male or female, are still inspired by him to work towards that goal.

Einstein conclusively proved that concepts of time and space which helped us organize our experience of the world were no longer scientifically valid. Discarding an intuitive understanding of time and space came with numerous advantages. Scientists after him gained a better grasp of the world at extremes. Together with engineers, they were able to push boundaries at both ends of the scales from the tiny (think of the electrons and photons that make our microelectronic devices work and which constitute our audiovisual culture) to the tremendous (such as the speed of signals traversing outer space and the monstrous masses in galaxies beyond ours). Consequently, common ways of making sense of everyday life were increasingly relegated to the arts and humanities. A world divided into the sciences and the humanities was productive—and dangerous.

Today Einstein's most speculative claims remain vibrant areas of research. He is still given chances not offered to any other scientist in history. Recent work on the existence of gravitational waves is a case in point. Much of the enthusiasm around their recent discovery with LIGO (Laser Interferometer Gravitational Wave Observatory) pertained to testing Einstein's predictions, ignoring the research on the same topic by others in his close circle. News headlines showered attention on the physicist, once again captivating numerous readers who had no reason to question the public benefit of spending millions of dollars to measure a minuscule change in the distance between two mirrors (about 1/10,000th the width of a single proton) to detect two imperceptible blackholes, that collided billions of years ago in a far corner of the universe.

In one sense, Einstein died a defeated man. Throughout his life, he had held grand hopes for science and rationality. Yet as he became the very embodiment of these virtues, his expectations were dashed. "By painful experience we have learned that rational thinking does not suffice to solve the problems of our social life," he told a gathering of utopian intellectuals who still strove towards the goal of creating a more peaceful world. Yet in another sense, he lived a successful life, honoring by example a dictum he was fond of quoting:

"The search for truth is more precious than its possession."

Suggested Reading

The secondary literature on Einstein is so voluminous that a good place to start is by reading his biographies in the order in which they first appeared. This way readers can get an Einstein that is temporally closest to him and farthest from ourselves. A compare-and-contrast reading strategy can reveal who Einstein was in addition to how he came to be. The first pages of the biography by Einstein's sister, which she began writing in 1924, have been reprinted in the first volume of *The Collected Papers of Albert Einstein*. Readers can also find in this collection the physicist's birth certificate, school records, correspondence from his mother and family friends.

The unauthorized biography by Alexander Moszkowski *Einstein the Searcher: His Work Explained From Dialogues with Einstein* (in the English translation) is interesting because of how much Einstein disliked it. The book appeared in 1921, shortly after Einstein became famous, and is temporally closest to some of the most important events that marked his life. Rudolf Kayser's first authorized biography *Albert Einstein: A Biographical Portrait* (1930) which appeared under the pseudonym Anton Reiser is a wonderful counterpart to Moszkowski's. Since it was written by the husband of his step-daughter Ilse who knew him well, it included intimate aspects of Einstein's life and personality that would become persistent themes in our understanding of him. Philipp Frank's *Einstein: Hist Life in Times* (1947) should come next on the list. The book is notable for placing the physicist's work in the broader context of the science and philosophy of his era and situating it in its political milieu. Although it was written by a friend and colleague of the physicist who shared much with him, its tone is less sycophantic and hagiographic than most other biographies.

Lesser-known aspects of Einstein's life are covered in these page-turners: *Einstein in Love: A Scientific Romance* by Dennis Overbye is the most well-documented and thorough investigation of the physicist's amorous relationships. *The Einstein File: J. Edgar Hoover's Secret War against the World's Most Famous Scientist* by Fred Jerome is a magisterial account of the physicist's life after WWII.

Beware of the fake news, fake quotes, and fake memes about Einstein, which continue to spread as they have done since 1919. For these, *The Ultimate Quotable Einstein* by Princeton University Press is the best antidote.

For scholarly accounts, Matthew Stanley's *Einstein's War: How Relativity Triumphed Amid the Vicious Nationalism of World War I* is unparalleled in its detailed attention to that period. *Einstein's Generation: The Origins of the Relativity Revolution* by Richard Staley helps us understand the physicist's contributions in light of others'. *Einstein's Clocks, Poincaré's Maps* by Peter Galison delivers a narrative situated in the techno-industrial context that was relativity's breeding ground.

Brave readers can tackle Einstein through his own popular and scientific writing. *Relativity: The Special and the General Theory* is still the best introduction to his scientific work. Two of his technical *Annalen der Physik* papers (both of which are the most readable *and* arguably the most famous) are widely available in German and in translation. My suggestion is to read them as bookends for his oeuvre: begin with the 1905 "On the Electrodynamics of Moving Bodies" (known for introducing the Special Theory of Relativity) and compare it against his 1916 "The Foundation of the General Theory of Relativity" (known for capping his efforts to generalize it).

For insatiable aficionados, the publicly available *The Digital Einstein Papers* offers the most comprehensive collection of his work and correspondence.

About the Author

Jimena Canales is an award-winning author and historian of science. Her books include *Bedeviled: A Shadow History of Demons in Science* (2020), *The Physicist and the Philosopher: Einstein, Bergson, and the Debate That Changed Our Understanding of Time* (2016), and *A Tenth of a Second: A History* (2011), which *The Guardian* named as one of the Top 10 Books About Time. Her essays have appeared in *The New Yorker*, *The Atlantic*, WIRED, and other journals. From 2004 to 2013, Canales served as an Assistant and Associate Professor in the Department of History of Science at Harvard University. From 2013 to 2017 she was the Thomas M. Siebel Professor for the History of Science at the University of Illinois, Urbana-Champaign, where she is currently on the faculty of the Graduate College.

A Word from the Publisher

Thank you for reading *Simply Einstein*!

If you enjoyed reading it, we would be grateful if you could help others discover and enjoy it too.

Please review it with your favorite book provider such as Amazon, BN, Kobo, Apple Books, or Goodreads, among others.

Again, thank you for your support and we look forward to offering you more great reads.

www.ingramcontent.com/pod-product-compliance
Lightning Source LLC
Chambersburg PA
CBHW030155100526
44592CB00009B/282